“THE MOST DANC

IN THE KINGDOM”

A History of William Pit, Whitehaven,
1804 - 1955

Ray Devlin
&
Harry Fancy

First Print:
August 1997

ISBN
0952681420

Published by:
The Friends of Whitehaven Museum

Distributed by:
Hills Books
Lowther Road
Clay Flatts Estate
Workington
Cumbria CA14 2DR
Tel: (01900) 603031/602781

Front Cover is Roundel from Cumberland Miners' Association Banner.
Photograph John Story, Whitehaven News.

Note: The date 1806 refers to the first winding of coal, not to the sinking of the pit

Printed by:
Miller Turner Printers Ltd., The Sidings, Beezon Fields, Kendal, Cumbria LA9 6BL

Contents

Appendices

Authors' Preface

This book has been produced as a mark of respect on the occasion of the fiftieth anniversary of the 1947 disaster at William Pit, and is dedicated to the memory of some three hundred men, women and children who lost their lives whilst working in "The most Dangerous Pit in the Kingdom"

As several of his forebears were Cumbrian colliers, it is fitting that Melvyn Bragg has contributed a Foreword to this book; we are most grateful for his apposite comments and the encouragement he has given to this project.

In compiling this study of an ill-starred pit, we have endeavoured to include a good deal of information which is not readily available in standard works, and we must therefore express our most sincere thanks to many individuals, too numerous to mention by name, who have been of assistance in this task. These include a number of former miners who provided valuable information either in the course of formal interviews or simply in the course of conversation. Particular thanks must be given to the miners Moses Stephens, Larry McCormick, Stephen Ferguson and Billy Turner.

Members of staff of the Cumbria Record Offices at Carlisle and Whitehaven have been unfailingly helpful, and Cumbria Library Service, Whitehaven News and Whitehaven Beacon have also co-operated by making reference material available for study. Unless otherwise specified, photographs were supplied by Whitehaven Beacon. Allan Routledge was most helpful in providing prints from photographs loaned for publication by many individuals. The poem reproduced as Appendix F was written and contributed by Mr. Frank Hewer, son of one of the victims of the 1947 disaster.

We must also express our gratitude to "The Friends of Whitehaven Museum", who financed this publication, with aid of sponsorship from The Coal Industry Social Welfare Organisation (Cumbria), and from Cumbria County Council's "Neighbourhood Forum" scheme.

Ray Devlin and
Harry Fancy, 1997

Foreword by
MELVYN BRAGG

Much of the history of this country over the last two centuries has been the story of thankless, grinding, often dangerous work in hard industries which drove on the economy and allowed all the great expansions - material and intellectual - of succeeding ages. The flowers of civilisation often had dark and bleak roots.

The basic industry for many generations was that of coal. For a long time most of the history of coal has been buried as deeply as the coal itself. Now it is a story which can be told in full and this book is a most welcome contribution.

My grandfather worked in the Cumberland coal field as did other members of my family and I used these experiences in a novel, "The Hired Man" part of which was set in Whitehaven. From my grandfather, from my own connections in West Cumbria and from the reading I have done over the years I think I have a clear view of the mining community that existed alongside the Solway. Its people had exceptional qualities - good humour despite frequent hardships, loyalty although so often let down, resolute in the face of constant exploitation. My father, who was born in Maryport always said that you did not know 'real' Cumbrian people until you went down West.

The William Pit could be described as central to the experience of this district since it was first sunk in 1804. Here we can read of profits being mined under the sea and largely taken out of the area for pleasures and investments way down south. Here we can chart the working and daily lives (virtually the same thing for many people) of all the thousands of men, women and often their young children who went down the mines throughout the years in conditions very like that of slavery. Here we read of a brilliant invention being tested - the Davy Lamp - and of overwhelming disasters occurring again and again. The story of this pit is the hitherto unsung, mostly unrecorded story of the lives of the majority of those who lived here before us. It is a book much needed, right for its time and I hope it will be widely read and supported.

Melvyn Bragg

Chapter 1

Historical Perspective

The Cumbrian coalfield covers approximately a hundred square miles, part of which extends beneath the waters of the Solway Estuary. The coal is of good quality, suitable for domestic use and for coke-making, but the purity and thickness of the seams deteriorates from the South to the North of the region.

These coal measures were systematically mined for a period of some three hundred years, although geological problems progressively reduced the viability of shaft mining during the Twentieth Century. Indeed, prior to its closure in 1986, the County's last deep shaft mine, Haig Pit at Whitehaven, had yielded a profit in only one year since Nationalisation in 1947. Today only opencast workings serve to remind us of West Cumbria's coal-mining past.

A Coal-Picker on the Beach, c. 1930

Fragments of "sea coal" can always be found on local beaches, particularly after storms, but local gleaners also gathered supplies from the pit "bank" (spoil heap).

Prior to the mid 16th Century, the very limited local demand for coal could be met by gathering from the beach or by extracting it from hillsides where seams outcropped on the surface. The first commercial exploitation of this natural resource seems to have occurred around 1560, when a company to extract and smelt copper was set up in Keswick by immigrant German miners. The supply of charcoal for smelting proved limited and expensive, so this was supplemented by coal obtained from Henry Curwen, Lord of the Manor of Workington. Teams of pack-horses were used to convey the coals some twenty miles overland to Keswick.

By the beginning of the next century relatively small amounts of coal were being exported from Workington and Parton to Ireland and elsewhere. Additional pits were being sunk at Clifton and Distington to help meet this market and to fuel local salt-pans and lime-kilns. The demand for coal was slowly expanding. However, the large-scale development of coal-mining was not initiated until Sir Christopher Lowther, second son of Sir John Lowther of Lowther, took charge of the Whitehaven Estate around 1630. This estate consisted largely of lands formerly owned by the Priory of St. Bees which had been seized by the Crown as a result of the Dissolution of the monasteries Acts (1536 & 1539). The estate had subsequently passed through the hands of Sir Thomas Chaloner and Thomas Wyberg before being acquired by eminent and wealthy Lowther family.*

Sir Christopher Lowther was uniquely qualified to appreciate the enormous possibilities which existed for his newly-acquired estate. Having operated for a time as a merchant in Dublin, he was well aware that the fast-growing city was faced by an ever-increasing fuel crisis. For strategic reasons, the English overlords had adopted a deliberate policy of de-forestation, whilst the country's coal reserves were sparse and expensive both to extract and to transport. Peat was extremely bulky and local supplies rapidly diminishing. The solution was to import coal directly into Dublin's harbour, and supplies were already being shipped from Flintshire, Lancashire and Workington. However, as Dublin mushroomed, demand continued to exceed supply. Christopher Lowther, with the wealth of his family to back him, determined to seize the opportunity.

It was clear that the existing small-scale extraction of coal in the Whitehaven area could not possibly satisfy Dublin's huge and growing demand: if he were to succeed in his aim, drastic measures would be necessary. New shafts would have to be sunk to exploit richer seams at greater depths; adequate arrangements would have to be made to transport coal from pit-head to harbour; a fleet of ships would be required, and the harbour facilities would have to be greatly improved. Above all, adequate manpower to achieve these objects was essential.

In 1566 an official survey of the "Crekes, Ports and Havens" recorded that Whitehaven then consisted of six fishermen's cottages and possessed but a single nine-ton vessel, "The Bee". The surrounding area was sparsely populated. This state of affairs had changed little by Christopher Lowther's time. He was confident that the lure of employment for miners and sailors would attract the necessary labour, both skilled and unskilled, but a building programme to accommodate this influx of workers would have to be undertaken. Churches, shops and public houses would also be required, and local agriculture stimulated to feed the growing population. Builders, joiners, metalworkers, quarrymen, brick-makers and other tradesmen flocked to the area, and they too had to be housed. So it was that as Dublin flourished, Whitehaven, and eventually other West Cumbrian ports developed in its wake.

* *It should be noted that in later generations the title 'Earl of Lonsdale' was bestowed upon the senior member of the family. For the purposes of this book 'The Lowthers' and 'Lord Lonsdale' are synonymous.*

Christopher Lowther was a man of action as well as of vision. He embarked upon his great project with boundless energy and application, determined to capture the lion's share of the lucrative trade with Dublin. Sadly, he was only to see the beginnings of this great transformation, dying at the tragically early age of 33 in 1640. His successors, in their capacity as Members of Parliament, were obliged to spend most of their time in London. Although 'absentee landlords', they were men of similar vigour, pushing forward the plans he had initiated, with the very capable assistance of Estate Stewards who conducted the day-to-day operations of the complex undertaking. Whitehaven became the first post-medieval "Planned Town" in England. Its numerous pits used the latest available technology; wagon-ways were constructed to convey coal to the greatly improved harbour where convoys of ships - built mainly in its own shipyards - awaited the tide.

At 966 feet, King Pit was at the time (1795) the deepest shaft in the world, whilst Saltom Pit (sunk 1729) was the first major under-sea colliery. The region's most brilliant mining engineer, Carlisle Spedding, who was Mining Steward to the Lowthers, invented the 'Spedding Wheel'* or steel mill, the first form of safety lamp, which was used in pits throughout the land for almost a century until superceded by the Davy lamp. During the sinking of Saltom Pit, Spedding was the first to use gunpowder for breaking up rocks. He pioneered the system of ventilation through the workings which later became known as 'Coursing the air', and in conjunction with Whitehaven's leading scientist William Brownrigg, proposed that methane, (the source of fire-damp the explosive gas found in mines) be used to illuminate street-lamps set up in the town. Almost two centuries were to elapse before 'natural gas' was used for this purpose. Brownrigg, a trained chemist, was the first person to investigate the nature of fire-damp, for which work he was elected as a Fellow of the Royal Society. Brownrigg also discovered that it is possible to predict the likelihood of pit explosions by observing barometric pressures; a rapid fall indicated a much-increased risk. Maintaining records of barometric pressure in coal mines became a mandatory practice, and remains so to this day. To speed the loading of collier ships, a huge bunker (a 'staithe') fitted with gravity-fed chutes (the 'hurries') was erected on the harbourside; this revolutionary device dramatically reduced the turn-around time of the vessels.

In such ways did Whitehaven attempt to keep pace with the demand for coal in Ireland, although rival entrepreneurs followed the Lowthers' example and were able to secure some share of the trade. It is against this background that at the beginning of the 19th Century, Whitehaven resolved to sink the greatest pit of its period. This was to be called "William Pit," and it was to be constructed almost adjacent to the well-equipped, bustling harbour.

* *The Spedding Mill consisted of a cranked gear-wheel which rotated a disc of hardened steel, against which a piece of flint was pressed. The stream of sparks thus generated gave a glimmer of light sufficient to permit a man to work. Although there was no continuous flame, the device was not completely safe and it is known to have caused explosions. Nevertheless, it was far safer than candles or other forms of lighting then available. See also Chapter 6.*

Chapter 2

The Owners and Lessees of the Whitehaven Collieries

For over two hundred years virtually all the pits in the Whitehaven area were owned and operated by successive generations of the Lowther family. During the early period, several relatively small inland pits were not considered worth adding to the Lowther empire and were worked by independent owners whose profits were meagre. Such small-scale workings were eventually either abandoned or absorbed into the Lowthers' holdings as they methodically extended their mineral rights in the area. Coal measures which lay beneath the sea were actually Crown property, but it was not until 1860 that a levy was charged for each ton extracted. Thereafter, the annual sum paid by the Lowthers averaged around £1,750 until 1880, when the then Lord Lonsdale purchased the Crown Rights for £50,000.

For a very considerable period the Lowthers had also leased the mining rights owned by St. Bees School, whose founding bequest included the rights to mine coal in the vicinity. From 1869, when this lease was re-negotiated, the school received an annual rent of £500 plus two pence for every ton extracted, and a "wayleave" charge for allowing coal to be transported over its boundary.

In the same year in which the Lowthers acquired the sub-marine rights, they decided that they would withdraw from mining entirely, as profits were falling. The pits, complete with their plant and equipment were leased to Messrs Bain and Company for an annual rent of around £14,000 plus two pence for every ton of coal produced. The company was controlled by Sir James Bain and his two sons, and J.S. Simpson, who was already the owner of the extensive iron works and a

Sinking Ladysmith Pit, 1902

Ladysmith Pit was sunk to exploit coal measures to the south of Croft Pit, whose old shaft was retained as the 'upcast' of the new mine. The headgear of Ladysmith is seen under construction on the right

coal mine at Harrington. To counteract the falling profits Bain & Co. introduced new methods of working and sunk a new shaft, the Ladysmith in 1900-02. This was done to develop undersea workings at the southern end of the measures. Indeed, from this time onwards, Whitehaven's output was almost entirely confined to sub-marine extraction. However, with some years of the lease still to run, profitability continued to be marginal, and in 1913 Bain & Co. and Lord Lonsdale agreed to terminate the arrangement.

The lease was taken up by The Whitehaven Colliery Company, for a fifty-year period. The annual sum paid to the Lowthers was to be £20,000, plus 4d, 6d or 8d per ton, according to the seam from which it was extracted. Shortly after the new company took over, the First World War commenced, with disastrous consequences with regard to the supply of manpower. In 1914 half the workers employed in the Whitehaven collieries (691 of 1,296 men) enlisted. Despite this manpower crisis the company immediately commenced sinking a new pit, patriotically named Haig, which was to dominate the output of the entire coalfield and destined to become the last shaft-mine working in Cumbria. The first shaft was sunk between 1914 and 1916, and the second from 1916 to 1918. After its closure in 1986 virtually all trace of the pit was removed, but a preservation order placed on its magnificent steam-powered winding engines ensured the survival of the engine house and one of the headgears. It is hoped to repair the somewhat dilapidated building and restore the engines to working order for viewing by the public.

Whitehaven's Screen Lassies

Traditionally, the widows of miners were offered employment as screen lassies. This photograph was taken in December 1962 to show the female workforce before the first redundancies were made at the year end.

The company was hit by a series of strikes in 1921, 23, 26 and 31, and numerous explosions resulted in the loss of many lives and costly recovery work. Despite the Whitehaven Collieries record output of 880,000 tons in 1927, overall production was falling; their output was never to approach this figure again. The imposition of a charge of five shillings per ton on coal imported into the Irish Free State in 1932 seriously affected Whitehaven's coal trade. Confronted by problems beyond its control, the company was accused of mis-management and in the following year its lease was terminated. The pits were then taken over by Priestman's Whitehaven Collieries Ltd. on a 99-year lease, commencing on 11th August 1933. The Lowthers were to receive an annual payment of £14,000 plus 5d, 7d or 9d per ton, according to the seams from which it was extracted. Priestmans made valiant efforts to improve matters, including much more effective 'screening' (cleaning, sorting and grading) of the coal and the securing of new markets.

In 1935 the removal of the duty on coals in the Irish Free State was greeted with enthusiasm. However, the Company appears to have over-reached itself with capital expenditure and was forced to close in the same year. Whitehaven's pits were idle throughout 1936 and did not re-open until leased by yet another concern - the Cumberland Coal Company (Whitehaven) Ltd. 1937. Again substantial investments were made, including pit-head baths, improved ventilation and a centralised system of power supply for pit operations.

During the first three years, until the commencement of the Second World War, production increased rapidly. Coal mining was designated "Essential Work," and colliers were exempted from military service. This did not prevent considerable numbers of them from volunteering, however, and by the end of the war a thousand less miners were working in Cumberland's pits than at its commencement.

The considerable distance which workers had to walk from the shaft bottom to the coal face meant the loss of many valuable man-hours each shift, so in 1939 one of the fastest available "man-riders" was installed at Haig Pit. This was a 350 horse-power Beckett and Anderson reversible endless rope hauler, which powered a man-rider on each of a pair of tracks. These carried workers a distance of three miles, at a speed of 15 m.p.h. The regulation speed limit of 8 m.p.h. was not imposed at Haig, and no serious accident ever occurred during almost fifty years it was in service.

After the war, Britain's pits were in a parlous state, run down, and with an increasingly aged workforce. To improve efficiency and reduce production costs vast investments in mechanisation were made, particularly after the Nationalisation of the coal industry in 1947. By this time Cumberland's collieries were seriously in decline. Most of the readily accessible seams were becoming worked out, and geological problems were thwarting efforts to introduce more advanced, highly mechanised

The Man-Rider at Haig Pit C. 1980

Because of the distance to the working face, special dispensation was made allowing these 'riders' to travel at 15 m.p.h. rather than the normal 8 m.p.h.

mining techniques. Setting up a working face for the 'long wall' method of mining using massive cutting machines is a major task requiring several months of preparation. Once extraction has commenced the investment of time and effort is steadily repaid, so long as the work continues without interruption. However, geological faults in the measures worked at Haig meant frequent adjustments in level in order to follow the seam, which seriously reduced efficiency and profitability. Sometimes the fault was so great that the face had to be abandoned and a completely new face prepared. The pit's cost-effectiveness steadily fell until it reached almost to the bottom of the 'league table'. The position was exacerbated by the fact that the market for coal was declining, too, as many heavy industries contracted and new forms of power - oil, natural gas and nuclear energy - came on stream.

In the light of the problems which existed within the Cumbrian coalfield, it is hardly surprising that local pits were closed, one by one. In 1986 Haig Pit ceased to draw coals, and two years later its shafts were sealed off and the pit closed; it was the end of an era.

Chapter 3

Planning the Pit

Since their acquisition of the Whitehaven estate, the Lowthers had methodically added to their land-holdings by shrewd purchases not only in the Whitehaven area, but at key sites to the North. Indeed, Sir James Lowther (1736-1802) - "The Bad Earl," stated that he was eager to "bid for anything on the coast from Whitehaven to Elnefoot, (Ellenfoot, Maryport)." This would give him additional mineral rights, and allow him to ship coal from various local ports, thereby increasing his control over the owners of collier vessels. His aim was "to increase or lessen the Trade at different harbours as I see cause." Thus the Lowthers were able to dictate and later to suppress, the development of Parton harbour. By the purchase of collieries at Seaton, Dearham and elsewhere, Sir James hoped likewise to control the harbours of Maryport and Workington. Later, considerable quantities of Lowther coal were indeed exported from Workington, to the chagrin of their arch rivals, the Curwens, who regarded this port as their own. These extensive land purchases also reflected Sir James' quite unfounded fear that Whitehaven's coal reserves were becoming exhausted; he was keeping his options open.

His Whitehaven land purchases were also strategic, but motivated by a somewhat different consideration - the savings which could be accomplished by increasing the scale of operations. By the physical linking together of numerous small pits, great economies could be made. Drainage and ventilation of the workings, for example, could be rationalised, and output transported underground to the most convenient shaft for winding. Alternative escape-routes would also be available in the event of a disaster, and in some cases unnecessary duplication of manpower and machinery could be avoided. For these reasons, the Lowthers had long coveted a tract of a hundred and fifty acres of land at Bransty, which bordered their Whingill Colliery. This estate had been held by various people, none of whom had chosen to mine the coal which lay below. It was not until 1781 that Sir James was able to purchase this land from Lord Egremont for the very considerable sum of £26,000. This gave the Lowthers the crucial missing piece of the jigsaw of land ownership around Whitehaven Harbour.

By coincidence, the year of the purchase saw the appointment of John Bateman (1749-1816) as general manager of the Whitehaven collieries. It was to be a somewhat turbulent period of managership, Bateman being dismissed in 1791, reinstated at a salary of £500 per annum in 1802, and again dismissed in 1811. It was during Bateman's second period in office that the sinking of the new great pit was planned and commenced. Despite the stormy relations which existed between the manager and his employer, Bateman was an extremely capable and energetic worker. The Bransty Estate offered the opportunity, and the challenge, of sinking a major new shaft on the North side of the harbour to exploit undersea reserves as yet untouched. His meticulous planning and execution of the project were ample testament to his abilities.

Between 1797 and 1800 James Pit had been sunk on High Street, close to St. James Church. Its output was conveyed to North Pier via a waggonway. An embankment at its lower end allowed it to cross the busy Tangier Street by way of a stone bridge - "Bransty Arch," which formed an impressive monumental entrance to the town centre. During the planning of the new pit, it was decided to drive an underground adit between the two which would facilitate drainage, ventilation and haulage. When this was accomplished, the winding of coal at James Pit, and its inconvenient overland transportation became redundant; coal mined at James Pit could be hauled directly to the new pit, thence to the harbour. Likewise, water from the higher pit could be drained to the lower for pumping. Indeed, the workings of all the pits in the Whitehaven area were eventually inter-connected in the interests of drainage, ventilation, access and escape routes.

The new pit on North Shore which was to be the 'flagship' of Whitehaven Collieries, would be equipped with "state of the art" technology. A point eight hundred yards from the harbour's north wall was selected for the sinking of the shaft, and the construction of William Pit commenced.

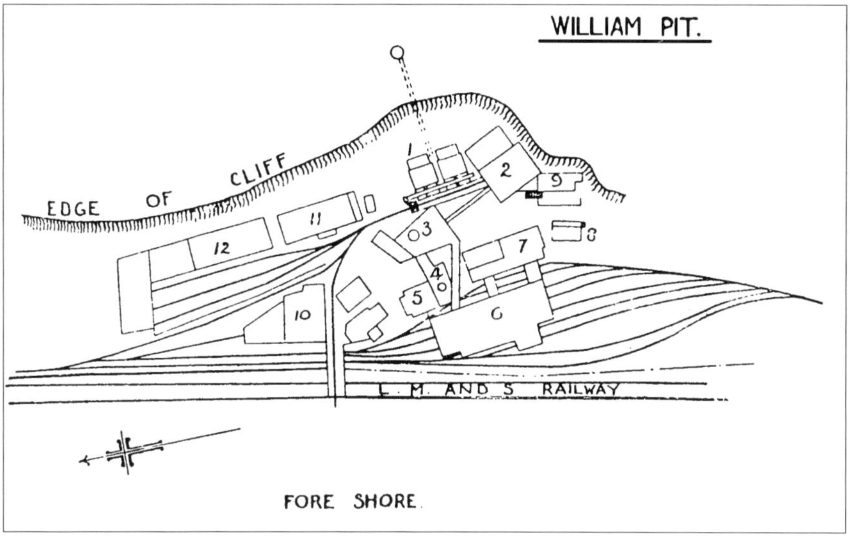

The General Arrangement of William Pit c. 1935

1. Boilers, Automatic Stockers, etc.
2. Winding Engine House
3. Coal Winding Shaft
4. Upcast Winding Shaft
5. Upcast Winding Engine
6. Screens & Dry Grading Plant
7. Stores etc.
8. Lamp Cabin
9. Office
10. Fan Engine House
11. Compressor House
12. Workshops

Chapter 4

Sinking the Pit

In a letter to Lord Lonsdale on the 23rd of January, 1804, John Bateman made a simple, yet historic comment -

"Your Lordship,

We are ready to begin sinking the new pit..."

Less than fifteen months later the initial task of sinking had been accomplished, to the astonishment of the mining world.

The following is an extract of a letter from an eminent Coal Viewer (who has seen the pit), to his friend in Whitehaven :-

"They have come on most wonderfully with the sinking of the new Engine Pit at Bransty. In the course of all my experience I have not met with any such important winning that was executed in so short a time, or anything nigh so short."

This fulsome tribute appeared in the Cumberland Pacquet Newspaper on the 26th of March 1805. The same article reveals the method adopted to achieve this remarkable feat.

Four teams, each of five men, worked six hour shifts in turn night and day, each team therefore working six hours in each twenty-four. They were given "liberal" wages, but in addition the entire team was set targets to achieve within a specified period. A sliding scale of reward was offered, the team receiving £16, £20, £24 or £40 to share according to the depth reached at each stage. On four occasions they received the maximum bonus. They were awarded an extra £16 on completion of the shaft in recognition of the fact that their work had been impeded at times by flooding and the presence of particularly hard strata of rock.

The shaft was fifteen feet in diameter and was sunk initially to a depth of 576 feet - extended shortly afterwards to 630 feet. The spoil was shovelled into tubs which were hauled to the surface using two horse-powered gin wheels* Each tub held forty gallons of spoil, and 55,803 loads were removed.

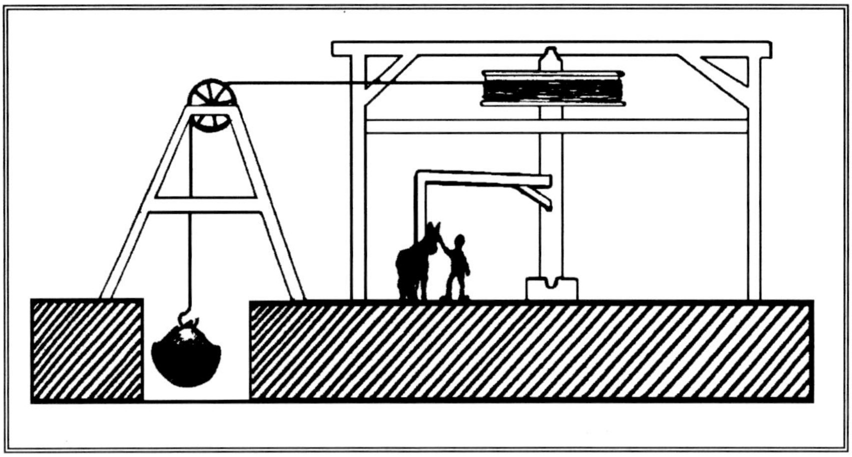

Whim-Gin

As the work progressed, a serious problem occurred when a considerable flow of water began to penetrate the shaft wall. Bateman rightly deduced that this was seeping from older workings in the vicinity, and acted quickly by installing a dam at the source. This greatly reduced the penetration of water, but before work could continue, the standing water had to be removed. In the absence of a pump, the teams were compelled to bail it into sixty-gallon tubs which were hauled to the surface. In all, 121,432 such tubfulls were extracted.

Another hazard was the pockets of firedamp encountered as they descended. These were usually ignited by the sinkers, a risky operation, which resulted in sheets of flame and sometimes minor explosions. A 'lamp' (fire) was kept burning at the bottom of the shaft at all times. In addition to giving much-needed illumination, this also generated a flow of air from the workings, thereby preventing any build-up of further firedamp gas which seeped from the walls. Much of the shaft passed through sound rock, but elsewhere it was necessary to line the wall with masonry. This operation, too, was carried out by the sinkers, who spent eight weeks on this part of their task.

Sinking commenced in May, 1804, and forty-six weeks later, on the 23rd of March 1805 the eleven-foot thick Main (or Prior) band was reached at 552 feet. This represents an average rate of twelve feet per week, accomplished in appalling conditions by men

** By this period the horse gin was of the type known as a 'Whim'. This device was consisted of a huge pully-wheel pivoted horizontally on top of a tall post. The wheel was rotated by horses which were hitched to beams fastened to the wheel above them, the number of horses used depending on the depth of the shaft and weight to be raised. The horses were thereby compelled to walk in a circle, so turning the wheel, which by means of a driving rope, rotated the spindle of the winding drum. At the end of a winding operation the horses had to be turned to reverse the motion of the drum, but later a reversing mechanism was devised.*

equipped only with hand tools but almost certainly with the assistance of gunpowder. It is a remarkable example of human determination and perseverance. Only one or two of the original team of workers who began it failed to complete the task.

The shaft was subsequently lined from top to bottom with timbers and divided vertically into three sections, two of which were to be used for winding men and coal up and down the shaft, the other for pumping water from the workings.

By November 1805 the "drift" (connecting passage) between William Pit and James Pit had also been completed, whilst pithead developments were proceeding. A double tracked, eight-hundred yard long waggonway to transport coal to the harbour was vital to the scheme, but its path was obstructed by a small hill, which, during the previous century had been developed as part of the harbour's defences. Fitted with a number of heavy cannon, this structure was known as the Jack a' Dandy Battery; the whole thing was levelled to the ground, its rubble, along with suitable stone recovered from shaft-spoil or quarried elsewhere, being used in the construction of the waggonway. To provide a level bed for the road, it was necessary to construct an embankment, which rose in places to fourteen feet above the natural lie of the land. As the presence of a substantial embankment and the continual passage of wagons along it would have denied access to shipyard properties on the seaward side of the track, a number of arches had to be inserted beneath the waggonway. This track alone proved to be a considerable undertaking.

The pit's coal yard was constructed to hold about 12,000 wagon-loads (22,000 Irish tons), and the engine-house and other pit-top buildings were erected. In keeping with the grandiose concept of the pit, its headgear was spectacular, consisting of a slender, truncated pyramid rising on four gigantic timbers. The newspaper article already referred to describes this unique structure, which was

> *calculated to answer a variety of purposes, viz., four large wheels, or pullies (sic) are fitted upon it, to receive ropes for two different rotative machines* two pullies, for hanging over the centre of the three divisions of the pit, so contrived, that a rope from a watch-gin may be changed from one division to another; also pullies for a capstan-rope for changing the buckets, spear rods, &c. This framing is of a pyramidal shape, upwards of eighty feet high, and at the top of it which is square, is very neatly ornamented, having four silver pheasants at the four corners, the four cardinal points of the compass, elevated from the centre, a large globe, and, above all, a figure of Mercury seven and a half feet in height, which, turning upon a pivot, moves with the wind, and, of course, acts as a vane.*

* *winding engines*

Sadly, there is no known painting or drawing of this remarkable pit-head structure which was surely unique in the history of mining. Even before it was erected and the first steam-powered winding engine installed, coal was being extracted by means of the horse-gins used for the sinking.

As soon as the Main Band was reached, the Cumberland Pacquet reported -

> *The vessel which took in the first coals from William Pit, is called the Lady Mountstewart, Hugh Ferguson, master, belonging to Bangor, in Belfast Lough, Ireland.*

The first winding engine, of forty-two horse-power, was installed in April 1806. This was built by Heslop and Millward at Seaton Ironworks, near Workington. It had two cylinders; the Hot cylinder 44 inches in diameter, the Cold measuring 28 inches, with a stroke of five-and-a-half-feet. It was to survive in use until 1850 when replaced with a much more efficient high pressure steam engine. It commenced drawing on the 10th of March 1806, and the first consignment of coal drawn in this way were put aboard the "Unity," William McDuff master. The pumping engine, erected in 1810 was a ponderous atmospheric engine with a cylinder of 82 inches diameter and a stroke of eight feet. It was rated at 100 horse-power and was able to lift 320 gallons of water per minute.

Although the sinking of the shaft had been accomplished with unprecedented speed, William Pit was not fully operational until 1812.

Chapter 5

Draining the Pit

It has already been seen that during the sinking of the shaft, the ingress of water from other workings had caused a problem. Much worse was to follow, when a considerable influx affected development work at William Pit for over three months. The following account explains both the cause of the problem and its remedy:-

Report by John Buddle and Thomas Ramsay on the influx of water from a trial in North Pit, South Whingill Colliery

Whitehaven Colliery, 25 November 1809

Being requested by the Earl of Lonsdale to view this colliery, in consequence of a large feeder of water having burst into the Whingill Division thereof, from the fissure in a dyke in West Trial from the South ends in North Pit.

We have examined the general plan of the Colliery, as also such parts of the underground as we found necessary to furnish us with the necessary information on the subject of our inquiry.

It is necessary to observe that the workings of this Colliery are in two divisions, which for the sake of distinction we shall call the Whingill or Rise Division, and the Howgill or Dip Division.

There is no communication whatever between these Divisions except by a stone drift 420 yards in length.

The feeder of water issuing from the fissure of the dyke as above stated, discharges an alarming torrent, but from the appearance and smell of the water together with other circumstances, we are fully of opinion that it is not a regular and natural spring, but that it is discharged from some old works, or other cavities, and that it must of course abate, if not entirely subside sooner or later. But it is impossible to ascertain when this may take place, prudence requires that the most effective measures should immediately be taken to place the Colliery in the most complete state of safety that its situation will admit of. The most effectual plan to secure both Divisions of the Colliery, is by fixing Frame Dams in the South Rolley roads and Thirl (passage?) immediately adjoining the fissure of the dyke from where the water issues in the North Pit, but we are doubtful that the dams cannot be made perfectly tight and secure in that situation, we strongly recommend Mr. Bateman's plan of fixing an effectual Frame Dam in the stone drift between the two divisions of the Colliery without delay.

By placing an effective Frame Dam in the stone drift, the Howgill or Dip Division of the Colliery will be completely secured, and as it is presumed that the old workings to the dip of the William, James, Lady, George and part of Davy and North Pits are sufficiently capacious to receive the feeder of water for about three months, there is time enough to endeavour to fix the dams recommended in the South Rolley Road and Thirl adjoining the orifice from which the water is discharged.*

As we have reason to believe that this feeder of water is discharging from the former old workings of the Six Quarters Coal which are not extensive, we are of the opinion that before the dam in the North Pit can be completed that that important fact will be fully ascertained, which of course render their completion unnecessary. At the same time we are by no means so confident in our opinion as to advise any delay in the completion of the Dams. We do not find it necessary to detail the plans of the different Dams and the manner of fixing them, here, as we have discussed the subject fully with Mr. Bateman and his parties who have to carry them into execution.

To conclude, we must observe that in our mind this accident has by no means arisen from negligence or want of attention, but on the contrary feel it incumbent on us in justice to the managers of the Colliery to state in our opinion everything has been done on the occasion which professional ability and zeal for the welfare of the concern could effect.

Signed: Jno. Buddle
Thomas Ramsay

Viewers from Newcastle.

This endorsement of Bateman's competency by two acknowledged experts must have been very welcome, but he was nevertheless to be discharged from his post by Lord

** A report by the Select Committee on accidents in mines, 1835 gives a description of Bateman's Frame Dam. It consisted of a heavy door, made from two or three-inch planks suspended from the top of a strong timber frame by means of hinges. A stanchion was set in place to keep the door raised when not in use. When it was necessary to close it, the stanchion was pulled away (probably by means of rope), so that 'the door fell down like a gun port lid'.*

Lonsdale less than two years later. Meanwhile Bateman and his men carried out the task of installing the dams, and by March the work was complete. The Cumberland Pacquet, 13th March, reported the celebrations :-

WHITEHAVEN COAL WORKS &c.

William Pit - On the fortunate event of completely restoring this Pit; which had from unforeseen causes, been inundated since about the middle of November last, by order of the Earl of Lonsdale, an entertainment was given at the Castle, on Saturday last (10th March) to the people employed in that work, whose exertions the Noble Proprietor was pleased to consider as highly meritorious; and, consequently, in his Lordship's opinion, deserving of particular notice; exclusive of the general festive meeting of the 20th January.

By persons employed in this work, as above mentioned, it is to be understood the Engineers, and those connected with them, viz. the Engine Men, Engine Fire Men (stokers), the Machine Men, Blasters (or Stone-Workmen) Water Strikers (men who built the dams?); Coal Viewers, Overmen, &c.

The entertainment, or treat, as it was called, to which the wives of all the workmen were also invited, consisted of a most plentiful Old English Dinner, of which upwards of eighty persons partook. During Dinner, a band of music played several popular airs, God Save the King, Rule Britannia, Britons, strike Home, Hearts of Oak, &c. &c. &c.

Dinner being ended, and after an interval, in which the glass was freely and cheerfully circulated, the Dance began; and in it so many joined as could. This was continued until the intrusive clock gave warning, that the 'Midnight Hour' was on 'The Point of Time'. The music ceased, and the company retired to their respective homes, preserving the same decorum which had been so conspicuous during the whole of the entertainment.

Having adverted to the circumstance which interrupted for a time the working of William Pit, we cannot help noticing in this place, that it gave rise to variety of false reports, some of which went so far as to prognosticate the utter ruin of these extensive coal works, whilst others asserted that the event had taken place, that a part of the town had sunk, several houses had fallen, and many lives had been lost, though, at the very same time, the other pits, both on the Howgill and Whingill side (William is on the latter) were working at a rate that, with the stock on hand, (which are called banks) was quite sufficient for the demand, and it providentially happened that not a single life was lost.

It is worth observing, that this Pit has been cleared of the water, before the grand engine which is to be applied to it, could be finished. This great work was chiefly effected by the Engine at Saltom, the excellency of which has been long known and acknowledged. And on this occasion, besides performing what might be termed 'its own duty', it did at least two thirds of the whole work, in conjunction with the smaller engines. The distance from William Pit to Saltom Engine is about a mile,

The damaged roofs, ways, &c. being completely repaired last week, and all cleared for business, the Agents completed the arduous task by regulating the air courses, &c. and yesterday William Pit began to raise coals as usual.

Great praise is undoubtedly due to all concerned in this work, for their skill, intrepidity, and exertion. Their Noble Employer has given repeated and indisputable proofs of his approbation, and the success which has crowned their labours on this occasion must be considered as a matter of great public interest.

The mention of this naturally leads to a remark on the astonishing change that has taken place in the town of Whitehaven, within the last seven years, where the value of property (in houses &c.) has increased, in several instances, even in a threefold proportion, and in which space of time, thousands have been added to its population, the further increase which is apparent in everything.

The report and the article clearly establish that underground workings of different pits were interconnected. In addition to the adit between William and James pits, the latter was linked to the much older North Pit on Harras Moor, where this and several other pits had been sunk during the previous century. In order to drain these workings a watercourse was driven from Bransty Beck, near the foot of Wheelbarrow Brow, to North Pit. This drainage 'level' was later extended to drain Jackson, Fox, Hunter, and Bateman Pits. North Pit could be entered via a 'bearmouth' (walk-in entrance) and due to the interconnection of the workings, it was possible to proceed though James Pit, eventually to enter the workings at William via the adit completed in 1805. Indeed, this route was used to lead the horses directly into William Pit rather than by lowering them down the shaft. If further proof were needed of the connection between North, James and William Pits, evidence given at an inquest into the death of a Mary Douglas is conclusive. Her body was discovered by a pit Deputy, whose duties included *inspecting the North Pit bearmouth as far as its junction with William Pit.* This inquest was reported in the Cumberland Pacquet newspaper, 3rd. May, 1842.

Saltom Pit c. 1860

Although no longer a productive pit by this period, Saltom continued to be used as a pumping station for much of the colliery. Some of the surface structures remain as a reminder of the first major undersea coal mine.

As already indicated, the inundation of water was removed from William Pit by means of the engine at Saltom, which continued to operate as the 'sump' for most of the local pits long after it had ceased to draw coals. Buddle's report stated that the only communication between the pits of the Howgill and Whingill divisions was 'a stone drift 420 yards. in length';. this had been driven right under the town in 1796. Once Bateman's frame dams were installed, the water coming from North Pit was diverted via the drift which ultimately led to the sump at Saltom. The water which had already penetrated into William Pit was removed using the small engine already installed there.

The newspaper article also makes it clear that considerable quantities of coal were being extracted from William before 1809. This implies that work on deepening the shaft must have continued whilst coal was being extracted from seams being worked above!

Chapter 6

VENTILATING THE PIT

As already intimated, the West Cumberland coal measures were particularly bedevilled by the presence of methane gas, which occurred in greater concentrations than in most British collieries. When mixed with oxygen from the air, methane forms the explosively inflammable gas **firedamp**. Despite the measures taken to control it, firedamp was the cause of most of the area's major disasters.

Spedding's 'Steel Mill'

The wooden handle used to turn the large cogged wheel is missing from this specimen in 'Whitehaven Beacon'. Until Davy's Safety Lamp became available, Steel Mills were used where candles were considered too dangerous.

Spedding's steel mill was an attempt to provide a safe light in these dangerous conditions. It was considerably less likely to ignite the gas than a naked flame, and by examining the colour of the sparks emitted, the operator was able to detect the presence of particularly dangerous concentrations, when the miners were withdrawn from the pit. Carlisle Spedding also pioneered the system of ventilation known as 'Coursing the Air,'* during the development of Saltom Pit. It had long been the practice to keep a fire burning at the foot of the shaft in order to produce a powerful updraft. This served to ventilate the immediate vicinity, but did not prevent the build-up of pockets of firedamp in remote parts of the workings. By dividing the shaft vertically into two sections he was able to provide an 'upcast' through which foul air was expelled, and a 'downcast', which allowed fresh air to enter. The clean air was then directed through the entire workings, flushing away the firedamp as it seeped from the strata. Although a significant development, coursing the air was by no means a complete solution to the problem. It was later refined by John Buddle of Newcastle, who arranged the management of the airways in such a way that different 'districts' of the mine could be ventilated at will. This technique was known as 'splitting the air.' Buddle did in fact visit Whitehaven colliery

** This system has also been attributed to Spedding's son James (1720-1788), who succeeded him as manager of the Whitehaven collieries. However, James was only a child when the method was first tried out at Saltom Pit.*

on a number of occasions and in 1835 in giving evidence before a Select Committee on Accidents in Mines, he reported that in the Lowther's pits "The system (of ventilation) adopted is one of the most completely managed mines that I know of."

'The Monthly Magazine' dated 1st June 1807 carried an article by Mr. Richard Philips of London which gives an interesting account of the state of mining in Whitehaven at the time, and gives a valuable side-light on the subject of ventilation. It is worth quoting in its entirety ;-

> *From the new system adopted in airing the Earl of Lonsdale's extensive coal-works near Whitehaven, the miners have fortunately been free from serious accidents for several years; although many new spreads or fields of coal have been opened out; and this process it is always deemed the most dangerous part of the service. The hydrogen gas, inflammable air* (actually, methane) *or dirt as the workmen call it, is now made useful in carrying on the works. They have collected a very large quantity of it, at the bottom of one of the upcast shafts* (Duke Pit) *and keep it constantly burning. The heat from it exceeds that of the largest coal fires, or lamps as they are called which are kept at the bottom of the upcast shafts, to rarefy the air in the pits. The speed of common atmospheric air, by burning the hydrogen gas, is greatly accelerated. It compels it to travel at the rate of more than four miles an hour; whereas common air, with coal fires at the upcast shafts, seldom sends it more than three miles an hour. It also saves the expense of attendance and coals which is very considerable at other upcast shafts.*

> *In these works, neither expense or care is wanting to make the situation of the colliers, whilst at their labour, as secure as possible; and they are accommodated with neat and comfortable houses, rent free, adjoining the town in the pleasant situation it affords. All the houses, in number 300,* (actually 266) *are supplied with excellent water, conveyed in lead pipes from the reservoirs made solely for their use above the level of the village. These houses are frequently whitewashed within to prevent infectious diseases; and annually on the outside also, which contributes much to the neatness of their appearance. From this improving state of these extensive works, all kinds of workmen, on their arrival, find immediate employment.*

Miners' Dwellings, Newhouses c. 1920

The three long rows of 'tied' cottages known as 'New Houses' were built in 1788 on the hillside alongside Preston Street between Newtown and Ginns. They were demolished in the 1940's.

This idyllic description of the dwellings is unrecognisable as the squalid, insanitary conglomeration of houses described by R. Rawlinson in his report to The General Board of Health concerning sanitary conditions, water supply, housing etc. of Whitehaven in 1849, but the references to burning methane to improve ventilation is interesting. It suggests that Spedding and Brownrigg's proposal to illuminate street lamps by its use was not as dangerous as the town authorities supposed at the time. It is also apposite to recall that right up to the time of its closure in 1986, Haig Pit's winding engines were still driven by steam generated from boilers in which methane gas from the workings supplemented coal and, later, oil. This was a safe practice, and made use of a natural resource that would otherwise have been wasted.

Despite all the coursing and splitting of the air, fires and explosions with loss of life occurred all too often, and attempts were made to use fans to provide ventilation. At Duke Pit a fan eight feet in diameter and four feet wide was installed in the up-cast shaft in 1840. Powered by a steam engine, this removed 23,000 cubic feet of air per minute, but for some reason it was used for only a few years. Perhaps the burning of methane was as efficient and far less costly! In 1844 a different form of fan known variously as a barrel-churn fan, rotary air drum or Fourness fan, was tried at Wyndham colliery, Cleator Moor. This proved moderately successful but the device was not adopted elsewhere.

It was not until 1870 that effective mechanical ventilation was introduced in the form of a huge Guibal fan was installed by T.E. Forster at Duke Pit. The enormous brick-built housing for this fan, although incomplete, and without the fan itself, is preserved in situ on the south side of Whitehaven harbour, along with other reminders of the town's mining heritage. These include the massive retaining walls of the Wellington Pit, the steps (albeit re-surfaced) which led to hundreds of miners' dwellings which once packed the terraced hillside, the lamp-house (now extended to accommodate the Coastguard Service) and the Howgill Incline. This was constructed by John Peile in 1813 to convey wagons of coal from the top of the hill to the staithes on the harbourside.

Duke Pit Guibal Fan Chamber

This historic building formed the upcast shaft of Wellington Pit. It was almost destroyed when the area was redeveloped in the 1970's. Fortunately, work was halted at this stage and the structure has been retained as an industrial monument.

So successful was the Guibal fan that it was gradually introduced in other pits. Fans of this pattern were installed at William and Kells pits by R.F. Morgan. Indeed, in 1889 the ventilation of William and its sister pit Henry (described elsewhere), was completely re-jigged; T.E. Forster reported that the furnace at James Pit, used to ventilate the Henry Pit, had been stopped. In future, the workings of both William and Henry were to be ventilated by the Guibal fan at the former. This spelled the end for James Pit, which had survived until this time mainly because of its role in ventilation. Production of coal at James had ceased many years earlier.

During the 20th Century the steam engines which drove the ventilation systems were replaced by electric motors. Whitehaven was, in fact, one of the first towns to install electric lighting, and the building which served as its generating station is also preserved on West Strand. Sensitively restored by North West Water in 1994-95, this pleasing Victorian example of industrial architecture was originally constructed as a sewage pumping station, but was extended in 1892-3 to accommodate a steam-powered generator which supplied the town with D.C electricity supply until the coming of the National Grid scheme in the 1930's. Whitehaven 'Beacon', a purpose-designed building was erected nearby to display and interpret the heritage of the area, and opened to the public in 1996.

Chapter 7

Working the Pit

In 1801, the year after the death of William Brownrigg, a collection of his writings was published by his close associate, Joshua Dixon, MD. Entitled "The Literary Life of William Brownrigg, MD, FRS", this rather rare book includes, amongst other things, an "Account of the Coal Mines near Whitehaven". Unfortunately it is not known when Brownrigg originally wrote this account, but it was probably during the second half of the eighteenth century. One passage gives an insight into mining procedures prior to the sinking of William Pit:

> *The following is the process of obtaining coals at Howgill colliery. After sinking a coal pit, or shaft, upon a new field of coal, which commonly costs about £10 per fathom (six feet); a level is first driven for 400 or 500 yards, in a north or south direction; and then a passage is cut through the several strata, to the surface of the earth, as a road for men and horses; and also to admit a current of fresh air into the mines. As the greatest care and judgement are requisite, especially when the works are infested with inflammable air; the best workmen are selected for this hazardous underiaking; as few people as possible are allowed to be in the pit, lest any of them should forget to shut the doors which they have had occasion to open; such a neglect, which undiscovered for a few minutes, has often proved fatal to every person employed. When these operations are finished, if the coals abound with firedamp, or with water, the pit is suffered to remain for many years without being worked. Where no danger, however, can be reasonably apprehended, the coals are conveyed from the bed to the bottom of the pit not by horses but by men, for greater safety, in a vessel in the form of a waggon, but only about a fourth of its size. Here they are discharged into baskets made of small rods, and containing about ten Winchester bushels; which are drawn up the pit to the surface, by one, two, three, or four horses, yoked to a lever, from 20 to 30 feet in length; which is connected with a vertical, or horizontal wheel, from 15 to 30 feet in diameter*. As soon as the basket appears at the top of the pit, one of the workmen pulls it towards him; and, the motion of the wheel being reversed, the rope becomes slack, and the basket which is suspended from the rope, rests upon a kind of sledge. It is then conducted to a place, near to the pit, where its contents are emptied. Two ropes, each about 4 inches in circumference, are fastened to the wheel, and so fixed that , while one rope ascends, the other descends: by*

** Brownrigg is describing a whim-gim. See page 16*

which contrivance the operations are carried on without any intermission. In such a pit, if it is sufficiently free from inflammable air, the following number of persons are necessary for the purpose of raising 160 baskets of coal in 9 hours (the same number of men and horses commonly work about nine hours in the day), at 100 fathoms deep.

8 MEN *to hew the coal, that is, to cut it out of the solid mine, and to break it to a proper size; in order that it may be conveniently taken into the baskets,*
2 WOMEN *to lift the coal into the baskets; each filling 10 baskets in one hour.*
8 BOYS *to drive 8 horses from the workings to the bottom of the pit; each horse carrying about 20 baskets in one day*
1 WOMAN, *at the bottom of the pit, to hook the full basket to the rope, and take off the empty basket.*
1 MAN, *at the top of the pit, to empty the baskets.*
2 BOYS *to drive the 4 gin horses* which are yoked to the vertical wheel.*

In the course of 9 hours, therefore, 160 baskets of coal may be obtained by the labour of 22 persons, and 20 horses; these baskets are equal to 20 waggons, according to the Whitehaven measure, or about 25 London chaldrons; and weigh from 42 to 44 tons. Where large quantities of coal are required, and the pits are few in number, it is usual, at the conclusion of the ninth hour, to have a fresh supply of workmen and horses. On some urgent occasions the period of labour has been limited to 8 hours; in which case, there have been three successive changes of men and horses in the same pit, within 24 hours. A horse employed in leading the coals upon sledges from the beds to the bottom of the pit, travels, where the roads are nearly level, about 9 or 10 miles during the time of its work. When the road has a rather perpendicular ascent, such as 4 inches in a yard, it travels only about 6 or 7 miles. Where the pits are of a greater depth, as King Pit, and Kells Pit, and where the stratum of earth, on which the superincumbent bed of coal rests, is very soft; the pillars, which are left as a support for the ponderous superstructure, are from 18 to 20 yards square; only about one third part of the coal, or four yards in breadth, being taken from the mine. Several of the present coal pits are constantly worked for above 50 years; but the first beds of coal have been long exhausted, to the rise of the shaft. The coal which remains, is principally below the level of the bottom of the pits, and at a considerable distance from them. About 18 or 20 years ago the daywork of a horse consisted in carrying only 8 baskets; which circumstance very much

* *After visiting Saltom Pit in 1739, Sir John Clerk, a Scottish colliery owner, noted that gin-horses were used in pairs, and worked shifts of eight hours - although their drivers, often boys and girls, normally worked twelve hours.*

increased the expense of obtaining the coal. To remedy this inconvenience, and to expedite the operations of the workmen, several of the pits were sunk below the coal, and levels driven until they intersected the beds of coal to the dip of the shaft. Waggon roads were then laid along these levels, and the coal was conveyed in baskets laid upon flat sledges. By this ingenious contrivance, one horse carries four baskets, instead of one according to the former practice: and travels one third greater distance. This plan was found to be attended with such a reduction in the expense of labour , that it is now generally adopted at Whitehaven, and also at many other collieries. The method of raising coals up the shaft by the power of steam engines, instead of gin horses, was, afterwards discovered to possess superior advantages in facilitating the necessary operations in the mines; and has, therefore, been since received into general use.

William Pit, in the Whingill colliery, was conceived on a far grander scale, and was to employ the best technology then available.

* * *

Miners on their way to work, c.1890

Groups of miners, with water-bottles hanging from ropes over their shoulders, pass the gasworks on their way to William Pit. The cliff to the rear of the site is clearly visible.

The seams of coal in the Cumbrian coalfield have a dip (downward slope) of one in twelve from East to West. The depth of the workings provided ample 'cover' between them and the sea-bed, so that it proved possible to mine under the Solway for as far as was economically possible. The workings from William Pit were to extend over three miles from the shore, and other pits (e.g. Wellington and Haig) were to penetrate still further. The workable seams reached by the William shaft were:- at 432 feet, the Bannock -Band (seven feet three inches deep), at 552 feet, the Main or Prior Band (eleven feet deep) and at 822 feet, the Low Seam (seven feet six inches). The Low Seam was generally refered to as the "Six Quarters Seam".

Only about one third of the available coal could safely be extracted, huge pillars some eighteen to twenty yards square being left to support the roof. The practice of "robbing out" such supports before abandoning a particular 'District' was extremely hazardous, but it was sometimes officially sanctioned, often with tragic consequences. The workings were made as regular as geological conditions would allow. A series of straight, parallel 'Roads' about four yards wide and up to twenty yards apart were driven progressively along the seam, to its full height. As these extended, similar roads were driven at right angles to the original ones, thus dividing the seam into rectangular blocks, somewhat reminiscent of the grid-iron pattern of the streets and buildings of Whitehaven town. This method of working was called the bord and pillar, or stall and pillar system. The intersecting passageways constituted the 'winnings' of the mine, and provided the means by which it was conveyed to the foot of the winding shaft.

At this period several methods were used to transport coal underground: it could be physically carried on the backs of low-paid workers (often women!) called 'bearers,'as remained the practice in certain Scottish pits until 1843; it could be dragged on sledges, or baskets placed on sledges; wheeled bogies could be used instead of sledges, and these could run on rails of timber or metal; if there were sufficient headroom, such bogies could be linked together to form trains ('rollies') to be drawn by horses; later, a system of rope haulage could be installed, in which steam engines provided the motive power.* As William was intended to be the most advanced pit of its time, bearers and sledges were never used, and women were employed only as horse-drivers. From the start, coals were hauled by 'Trailers' from coal face to the rolly-road in 'corves' (baskets) placed on trams. There the corves were lifted by means of small cranes onto larger trams which were hauled, several at a time, to the shaft by means of horses. All the rolling-stock ran on iron rails.

In planning this prestigious new pit, Bateman's main consideration, of course, was efficiency. Labour, whether of men, women and children, was expensive and he made every effort to substitute horse-power for man-power, and steam engines for horses - for these were expensive, too. Horses had to be purchased or hired, and the cost of feeding one for a week was equivalent to a collier's wage. Their drivers also had to be paid. In view of these factors, horses would replace human workers *only where it was economic to do so; engines would replace horses only where worth-while savings were to be made.* The drive to substitute machines for men is nothing new. The practice at William Pit and elsewhere, became a calculated balance between manpower, horses and machines.

* *In more recent times, electrically-powered conveyor belts became the norm.*

Corves in use at William Pit, 1868

William was possibly the last pit to use corves for haulage purposes. One corf has just been raised up the shaft; it will be lowered onto a bogie for removal to the staith, like the one seen to the left.

Baskets called 'corves' were used as containers in which coal was moved. These were woven from stout hazel rods and were made in different sizes. The smallest were used in conjunction with light wooden bogies to take coal from workface to the 'rolley road', where they were placed in pairs on larger 'trams,' several of which were coupled together to be taken to the shaft bottom by horses. There, the small corves were tipped into much larger ones, each containing 13 cwt, which were hauled up the shaft by steam-powered winding engines. Until cages were introduced, the mine-workers also descended and ascended the shaft in these baskets. Astonishingly, this archaic method of winding continued to be used in William Pit until at least 1875, possibly the last instance of their use in British collieries.

Bateman was firmly in favour of using durable iron rather than wooden rails for bogies, and between 1802 and 1811 he was responsible for making this substitution in many of the local pits. Lord Lonsdale's extensive iron foundry was almost entirely occupied in producing replacement rails for a period of several years. After Bateman's time, a new form of haulage was introduced into William Pit, when in 1818 a high pressure stationary steam engine was erected underground. By this time some of the workings extended a considerable distance, and the incline was so arduous that horses were barely able to cope with the task. Instead ropes, first of hemp, later of wire, were attached to the rollies which the engine drew to the shaft. This system was used only for long-distance haulage; elsewhere in the pit, horses remained in use for a considerable time. It must be stressed that these really *were* horses, not mere ponies.

The Whitehaven News reported on 19th September 1872 a court case in which eleven boys employed as drivers in William Pit were charged with neglecting their work in the pit and in the case of two of them, of having their safety lamps unlocked in contravention of the safety regulations. In giving evidence, William Harker, Overman, stated that the boys had released the horses and were "going to play at circuses". The Magistrate, Mr. Jefferson, demanded "Can little boys like that (pointing to one of the smallest) manage a horse 15 or 16 hands high?" "Yes, Sir," the witness replied, "he could a great deal better than some men." It is known from other sources that large Clydesdale horses were normally used in William Pit.

It was as a result of the First Coal Mines Act of 1843 that female labour underground was totally prohibited, and no boy below the age of ten could be thus employed. As a pit-owning Member of Parliament, Lord Lonsdale was certainly aware of the implications of the Act well before it was passed, and hastened to ensure that his pits would comply with the new regulations.

In preparation for the Act a team of Commissioners toured the coal-mining districts of England, in order to investigate the extent and nature of child labour. The following references to pits in Cumberland appear in their report :-

> *In this district the height of the coal-seam admits of horses being brought up to the workings; and in all Lord Lonsdale's Collieries, and in the larger mines in general on the coast of Cumberland, the coal is drawn by horses directly from the workings to the shaft. In these coal-mines, no Children or Young Person are employed in trailing, hurrying or putting. Still the evidence shows that there are mines in which Children are employed as trailers; but these are stated to be chiefly in the smaller and inland collieries. In the coal-mines in which trailers are employed the Children have to help to fill and riddle the coals as in the Yorkshire District.*
>
> *Trappers are employed in nearly all the pits, and their work is somewhat augmented by having occasionally two or more doors to have to attend to, and by having to alter checks,('points') so that the trains may pass along their proper roads at the dividing places. But the chief employment of Children and Young Persons in the coal mines of this district is to drive along the tram-ways the horses which draw the trams of baskets loaded with coal, several of which are hooked together. The journeys along these tram-ways are greatly lengthened, owing to many of the large collieries being sub-marine. In the William Pit they have 500 acres under the sea, and the distance is 2 miles and a half to the extreme part of the workings. There is a stable also under the sea in this immense pit for 45 horses. The shaft is 110 fathoms (660 feet). A feature exists in this driving employment I have not hitherto seen, and which constitutes the chief labour of the occupation. To prevent the baskets from running downhill and falling on the heels of the horses, it is customary for the driver to place himself as a post between the foremost basket and the buttock of the horse. He places the left shoulder against the horse, the right foot on the rail of the tram, and the right hand on top of the basket; the left leg being generally supported by the trace. When a train of corves is heavily laden, or the descent very steep, a pole is placed*

through the hind wheels of the trams, and thus it is in a measure dragged. Nevertheless the work is very toilsome, and, as will be seen from the evidence of the surgeon attending Lord Lonsdale's collieries, accidents sometimes occur by the foot slipping off, and getting struck by part of the wheel or axle. The leaning position in which they stand is not in itself, I think, injurious; but the work strikes one as being palpably unnecessary, and as a barbarous preference of the human body for a mere mechanical process; in which shafts might be, and in some of the inland pits are, used instead ....

In most of Lord Lonsdale's extensive collieries they work night and day - the shift who work twelve day-hours one week working the twelve night-hours the succeeding week, and so on alternately . The appearance of the adults in these collieries was remarkably pallid and emaciated. I should attribute this greatly to the system of night-working; and there is a probability that the change from night to day-hours operates more unfavourably on the health than it would do if they were to work altogether at night. In the latter case habit becomes second nature, and sleep as refreshing is obtained by day as by night. Not so when the animal system is subjected to continual change, no habit is formed, and according to the evidence the rest obtained in the day is very deficient; so much so, as to render the night-work irksome through the inclination for sleep. The wife generally goes to bed by day with her husband, and so do all the family, and the door is often fastened to preserve as much quiet as possible. In some few pits eight hour shifts are worked. (Report by J.C. Symons) †*

The full text of the Cumberland section of this report appeared, with additional data, in a large article in the Cumberland Pacquet Newspaper, 7th June, 1842. Some other points made were that although children as young as eight and a half were sometimes employed in local pits, ten was the usual starting age; they worked the same hours as adults - generally twelve hours, and in some cases up to fourteen; at six to twelve shillings per week, their pay was regarded as 'good' (adult colliers, whose work was different, were paid eighteen to twenty-five shillings a week); the children received virtually no education whatsoever and were "as ignorant as it is possible to conceive children to be." The report also stated that only one old pit belonging to Lord Lonsdale still employed female labour underground. Before the Act was passed, His Lordship had conducted his own survey of the workforce and ensured that it complied rigorously with the new regulations.

Had such a survey of child labour been conducted thirty years earlier it would have included a considerable number of steel mill operators who were often the very

* *Sunday, a non-working day, intervened between the change-over of shifts.*

† *The full text of the report as it appeared in the Cumberland Paquet is reproduced as appendix C.*

youngest members of the workforce. In those parts of the workings considered too dangerous for candles to be used, it was their task to crouch beside the face-workers, constantly turning the crank of the mill to provide a glimmer of light. This work of utter monotony continued virtually without interruption throughout the long shift, often for several years, before the children graduated to other tasks. However, this class of worker was entirely eliminated with the introduction of the true safety lamp. Following Bateman's dismissal in 1811, his former deputy, John Peile, was appointed as the Lowthers' mining manager. Peile was to have a long and outstanding career, and it was he who in February 1816 arranged for the lamp invented by Sir Humphrey Davy to be tested in William Pit, and shortly afterwards its adoption in all the Whitehaven pits. In July 1816, his letter to Davy included the following remarks :-

> *With us the general use of the lamps, in consequence of the good state of our ventilation, is confined to the leading workings, or trial drifts; and in two of these, lately going on in one of the pits usually infected with firedamp, and which were previously lighted by means of steel mills, we applied the lamps with great confidence and security.*
>
> *In May last, in these drifts an extraordinary discharge of firedamp burst from the pavement of the mine, and the ventilation being at that time unavoidably obstructed, the atmosphere became so charged with fire-damp as to be nearly throughout an explosive mixture. In this situation we derived the unspeakable benefit of light from the lamps, and, notwithstanding the explosive state of the mixture, with the most perfect safety*
>
> *....By experiment, a pint of oil, value sixpence, will supply a lamp for six days, the ordinary time of a man's working, so that they are cheaper than candles....If my humble testimony can in any degree promote the speedy use of the lamp in other places, it will give me great pleasure....*

Peile's reference to candles is interesting. Elsewhere in the article he reveals that candles were still used in parts of the pits considered 'safe.' Indeed, it was not until late in the century that miners were prohibited from removing the tops of their safety lamps to give more light until they reached their working areas - the main roadways were believed to be so well ventilated that no danger existed. Another very dangerous practice was to use pieces of discarded winding rope, soaked in oil, as a form of candle. This was referred to as "Low Rope", and in 1803 Bateman reported with great concern that miners were using these improvised lights at Lady Pit.

* * *

Coal-Screening Plant at William Pit, 1911

Several 'Screen Lassies' can be seen looking at scores of trucks in the crowded marshalling yard.

Although the opening of this major new pit was essential to keep pace with Dublin's increasing demand, it could not have occurred at a worse time with regard to the available workforce. The Napoleonic Wars had led to the conscription of vast numbers of able-bodied men, and many trades, including mining, had been seriously affected by this move; labour, particularly skilled labour, was in short supply. In 1808 Bateman reported that almost a fifth of his 'haggers' (face-workers) had been lost due to a recent epidemic and compulsory service with the militia. Collieries in various parts of the country attempted to induce men from other areas to join their workforces. The Lowthers at Whitehaven and the Curwens at Workington were guilty of covert 'poaching' of each others' workers. Whilst the Workington pits offered higher wages, Lowther's miners were provided with free housing and coal; many workers migrated periodically from one to the other. In Newcastle, virtually all miners were 'bonded,' being paid substantial sums (ten to fourteen guineas) to sign a written contract to serve for an eleven month period. Until 1799, Scottish miners were in effect bound to their pits for life, without any such payment. Cumberland pit owners placed advertisements for workers in Newcastle and Scottish newspapers, and also in Manchester, with a little success. Considerable numbers of unemployed, unskilled Irish workers flocked to the pits, but relatively few were taken on at that time.

This shortage of labour around the turn of the century led to agitation for higher pay, demands which were backed by threats of strikes or of moving elsewhere. Reluctantly the owners agreed to some increases in pay. In 1802 Bateman ruefully commented "the men are all become Masters, and more Money is given for work than it deserves, & they get drunk with the Overplus." He countered by stepping up his efforts to obtain more workers, reasoning that "having men to spare will be the first thing to quiet the ones we have." He also succeeded in introducing 'Binding' contracts similar to those in Newcastle into all the pits in Whitehaven except for the newly-completed James Pit. This quickly proved unenforceable and he was compelled to abandon the scheme after the expiry of the first eleven-month contracts. In 1811 the Whitehaven miners established a short-lived Trade Union in defiance of Parliament's "Combination Act" which made such bodies illegal*

* * *

Although William was arguably the best-planned and equipped pit of its era, it was necessary to effect improvements from time to time in order to keep abreast of new technology. One of the greatest of these developments stemmed from the increasing complexity of its workings, and the distance of its workface from the shaft. In 1870-72 a new pit, the Henry, was sunk to a depth of 930 feet immediately adjacent to William. This was designed to work seams under land to the East - formerly exploited by the defunct James Pit and others - and seaward below those worked from William. A description of Henry Pit appears in the Whitehaven News, 6th June, 1872 :-

THE WHITEHAVEN COLLIERIES
WILLIAM PIT

Of late years, the improvements in these collieries have been varied and extensive. Not long ago we had the satisfaction of announcing the erection of one of Guibal's fan ventilators on the south side, on the shaft known as Duke Pit, whereby to discharge Wellington Pit of its impure air (see chapter 6). *Other improvements have been made in this colliery, but these must be the subject of another paper, as what we are about to notice now are the workings on the north side. The north side we visited the other day, and had the pleasure of inspecting the whole of the works, both above and below the ground. On arriving at William Pit top the first new work brought under our observation which has lately been put down immediately adjoining the old one.*

This is perhaps one of the finest shafts in the north of England, being circular in shape, 12 feet in diameter, and 153 fathoms (918 feet) deep. It has lately been completed, and a couple of drifts are being driven, one in a north-westerly direction, and the other in an opposite course. This pit will

* *This was quickly crushed, and another attempt to form one in 1831 came to nothing; the miners were instructed to sign a declaration that they would not join, on pain of dismissal. They refused to sign and commenced a three-week strike, at the end of which they were obliged to capitulate. In 1843 P.M. Brophy, a Delegate of the Miners' Association attempted to induce Cumberland miners to form a union. This resulted in a six-week strike, riots and the intervention of troops and Special Constables. The embryonic union was aborted and its leaders dismissed. It was not until 1868 that a Miners' Union was successfully formed in the county.*

in future be known as the Henry, as it is called after the Christian name of the present Earl of Lonsdale. The object of putting down a shaft is to enable His Lordship's engineers to get to what is called "six quarters coal." This is a seam of coal which has already been proved, in both William Pit and Wellington; it is some six or seven feet in height, and 45 fathoms (270 feet) below the Main Band, which is at present being worked.

In order to get the coal, a straight drift, about a mile in length, has been commenced, and although the coal will be come upon before that distance is reached, the ultimate object is to get a communication with the present workings, which will be done by sinking a small shaft from the Main Band into the Six Quarter, and lowering coals into the latter, and hauling them by engine from the top of Henry Pit, and so do away with a great deal of horse labour at present in use. While able to work the two seams as well as both shafts, it is expected that the pit will produce at least twice the quantity of metal (coal) she is now doing and considering the demand for Whitehaven coal is daily becoming much greater than the supply, the additional quantity will be gladly welcomed by consumers.*

At present the new shaft is worked with a small winding engine, with wire rope and an iron kibble, and as the sides have not yet been put in, the ride up and down is anything but a comfortable one. These will shortly be replaced by a horizontal engine with two 32 inch cylinders, three boilers 8 feet by 30, and the necessary riding gear. The site of the engines will be immediately adjoining the present reservoirs which supply the pit with water, and in order to make room for them, new reservoirs are being put down opposite the old gas works, and as soon as they are ready to receive the water the old ones will be closed, and the engines and engine house commenced with.

On proceeding down the old shaft we found that the basket is still in use there, and doubtless, with the appliances as command, it is quite as safe as the patent safety cage. This shaft was completed in 1806, and the bottom is reached at a depth of 103 and a half fathoms (621 feet). Arriving there we proceeded under the guidance of Mr. Robson, one of His Lordship's mining engineers, and John Rothery, the master wasteman, accompanied by Mr. Mills, a pupil of Mr. Forster's, Lord Lonsdale's consulting engineer, towards the workings.

The first part of the journey was on foot, and the locomotion was anything but disagreeable even to the uninitiated. There was a good road, plenty of

** The term' metal' is here used to signify coal; later its meaning was reversed, indicating stone - hence 'Metal Band' was the name given to a stratum of rock within the Main Band seam of coal.*

headroom, capital ventilation, and all that could be desired in a coal mine. The first stoppage was at a station where horses which work the rolley-road are supplied with water, and a train of empty carriages was waiting ready to receive us, and transport ourselves further into the bowels of the earth. We may well explain that our carriages were not the same pattern as those used on our present railway system above ground. They were simply empty coal baskets that were used for hauling out the coals, and capable of holding not more than two persons. Seated on the bottom of one of these, accompanied by one of our party, the other two having a basket between them, the driver got orders to proceed, and off he started at a decent pace, whistling a merry tune as he went.

About a mile by rail brought us to the lamp station, where the man in charge locked our lamps and took possession of our pipes, then we hied on to what is known as the Delaval district. On our way we looked into one of the stables, and found it to be very clean, with white-washed walls, and the stalls as pure as hands could make them. The horses were all in capital working condition, and, unlike most pit horses, received good characters from the stablemen. The horses are mostly low, thick-set powerful animals of the Clydesdale breed, and some of them when purchased cost as much as £70 and £80 a head. On renewing our journey we were not long in reaching the workings, which were situated some 5,000 yards under the sea from the bottom of the shaft.

The first place we arrived at we found a couple of "haggers" at work, and there we secured a section of the face, which is as follows :- Main top, two feet six inches; parting, half-inch; lyre coal, or undergrowth, one foot three inches; parting, half-inch; lying on coal, six inches; black stone, two inches; spar coal, one foot; bank coal, three feet; presenting altogether a face of eight feet six inches (i.e. Main Band comprised several seams, each given a specific name, separated by thin layers of stone). *The roof, which requires little or no timber, is what is called the bearing-top coal, one foot eight inches in thickness; and above that there is a parting of one inch and ten inches of little top, a foot of "cash", and ten fathoms* (sixty feet) *of "post" roof. The size of the working would be about five yards wide, and had good air, right up to the face, and in answer to a query put to one of the men, he said they were clear of gas. In fact, one of our pilots said he could not show us any gas in William Pit; not that she did not make any, but the ventilation was so good that foul air could never accumulate.* (Would that his confidence had been justified!) *Several workings of a similar nature were visited in this district with the same result. The Forster workings, which at present extend 6,000 yards from the shaft, or about three and a*

William Pit Screen Lassies

Theses women workers had their own "canteen", which was always refered to as the "Bait Cabin"

quarter miles in a north-west direction from Redness Point, as well as the Nova Scotia district, are worked in a similar way and the whole of the coals are brought to the bottom of the shaft by horses and trams, the number of animals being employed below ground being 84. When once the drift from the new shaft is completed, and a connection is made between the two seams, a great deal of horse labour, which is very expensive, will be dispensed with, and most of the haulage will be done by an engine with wire rope from the top. At present there are about 420 men and boys employed, and the cost of labour alone is nearly £1,000 a fortnight. Having visited several other places of interest, the return journey was commenced, and upon reaching the lamp station, we again joined the railway, and after a somewhat uncomfortable passage, caused by the jolting of the trams, we returned to bank, glad once more to see the blue vault of heaven.

The whole of the works are under the management of Messrs T.E.Forster and Son, who have as resident engineers Mr. Harper and Mr. Robson, and the systematic way that everything is carried on reflects credit upon all.

Henry Pit was ventilated via the up-cast of James Pit which was maintained for this purpose until 1891 (see chapter 6) by which time the Whitehaven Collieries had been leased to Bain & Co. In that year the leasees embarked upon a major re-development at William. Henry ceased to draw coals, its shaft being converted into the down-cast for William, a huge Guibal fan had been installed at the William shaft and now ventilated the combined workings. This process of rationalisation culminated in driving a new underground haulage plane in 1900-1901. This was reported in detail in the Whitehaven News, 17th October, 1901:-

William Pit, Whitehaven

Important Haulage and Ventilation Changes

Opening of the new Haulage Plane. October 1901

During the past week the first portion of a most important undertaking has just been completed and opened out for haulage and ventilation purposes at the William Pit, Whitehaven Collieries, which is sure to have a pleasing and far-reaching effect not only to the owners and managers, but also to the workmen and everyone concerned. William Pit has been working almost continuously since the year 1804, and "Old Father Time" has marched on, necessitating changes in haulage, and ventilating roadways, as well as in other branches of our great mining industry; and for some time it has been under consideration to re-construct the entire haulage arrangements to facilitate the work of the colliery, and to prepare for the ever-increasing demands of such an extensive area as prevails at William Pit. It was decided to drive a new engine plane for this purpose, which, when completed, will be practically in a straight line with the shaft bottom, and will extend from four to five miles in-bye, and the first length of this enormous undertaking has just been completed and connected, measuring 1,456 yards, and 400 yards driven seven years ago - 1856 yards already completed in this great undertaking.

The drift in its finished size is 12 feet wide and 10 feet high, the roof and sides where necessary being secured by semi-circular brick arching, or brick side walls and steel girders, and substantial larch bars and legs. Two lines of rail are laid, 2 foot 6 inches gauge, with 4 feet between the rails for travelling, and electric signals are fixed in the centre of the drift. Some idea of the enormous amount of work accomplished may be gathered from the following particulars :- About 540,448 cubic feet have been extracted; nearly 60,000 tubs of debris filled and sent out of the pit.

Thousands of tons of bricks and slag lime, steel bars, larch bars , cover wood &c. have been sent down the pit to secure the roof and sides. Over 20 tons of explosives (roberite and gelignite) and nearly 60,000 detonators have been used, and it is computed that nearly 30,000 shots have been fired without a single accident from explosives.

Over 30,000 sleepers, and 970 eighteen-feet rails, and 3,880 fish bolts, 1,940 fish plates, nearly 20,000 dog spikes, 145 roller pulleys and wood boxes, 290 brackets, and 1,150 8″ and 10″ bolts &c. have all been to handle and fix, without a single ton of coal being lost to the pit, the extensive working department in-bye proceeding as usual, and the daily output of 1,200 tons of coal per day average being fully maintained, although the new plane at two points abuts onto the old engine plane, now defunct.

The in-bye end of the new plane is some 12 feet above the out-bye end vertically and this has enabled the drift to be driven at a slight inclination in favour of the load, the in-bye end terminating at a point known as Hinde's *drift, and not the least interesting feature connected with the new plane, is a splendid curve, which has been specially designed, and put down by the management to connect the new plane onto the old plane beyond.*

There is difference in the direction of the two engine planes at this point of 32 degrees, and the curve has been designed to connect the two, and is fit up with special steel pulleys, with the bracket frames fixed at an angle of 30 degrees from the horizontal, and securely bolted onto pitchpine logs; The pulleys are 3 feet in diameter, and have been designed to supersede the easily displaced Tee pulleys, which are so ruinous to the life of the haulage rope; each pulley is fitted with a lubricating cup, and the whole job complete is a decided success; the bogies with rope in clutch, passing around smoothly and with never a hitch. The whole drift was let to Mr. Roland Williams, 1, Bransty Villas, Whitehaven, and he commenced the work on February 10th, 1900, and the ropes were coupled up and the sets (trains of tubs) *running through on* October 6th, 1901. *It will thus be seen that 1,456 yards x 12ft. wide x 10ft. high* (finished size) *had been driven, secured, and completed in 86 weeks or 602 days, which is equal to 2.4 yards per day of 24 hours, or 37.4 cubic feet per hour extracted. This is the second drift Mr. Williams has contracted for at this colliery, and it says much for the satisfaction he has given his employers that the continuation of the new plane beyond has also been given to him.*

It should also be mentioned that the work was done in two sections, 954 yards being driven from the out-bye end, 502 from the in-bye end to meet each other, and it must be specially pleasing to the colliery surveyor, who surveyed and levelled for the new plane, that the work throughout has been so accurate. Much satisfaction must also be felt by the owners, and by Mr. Turner, the manager, also by the under-manager, and other officials, that the result of their united labours, and the energy, tact, and vigilance exercised have been so abundantly, and pleasingly rewarded, and the finest engine plane extant such a decided success.

The continuation of the plane was accomplished without incident, but the cost of this massive and necessary undertaking stretched the capital resources of Bain & Co. to the limit; in 1913, their lease of the collieries was terminated.

Chapter 8

An Early Visit to William Pit

In 1813 the writer Richard Ayton (1786-1823) and the artist William Danniell (1769-1823) embarked upon a project which was not to be completed until two years after Ayton's death; it was not until 1825 that the last volume of their book "A Voyage round Great Britain" was published. The complete set of eight volumes was lavishly produced, contained no less than 308 aquatint illustrations, and sold for the then enormous price of £60.

It is often referred to simply as Danniell's voyage, since Ayton seems to have dropped out of the partnership shortly after their visit to Whitehaven in 1814. Thereafter, Danniell continued with the project alone. Whilst the quality of his illustrations remained exceptionally high, his writing is not nearly as perceptive or fluent as that of his partner.

It is indeed fortunate that Ayton was involved with the project long enough to record the following account of their visit to the recently-opened William Pit This remains one of the most graphic and disturbing descriptions ever written of actual working conditions in a British pit at the beginning of the 19th Century:

> *Having seen all operations connected with coals above ground, I was determined before I left Whitehaven to descend down one of the pits and see the wonders below. A gentleman of the place, who had himself frequently made the experiment, and who from his knowledge was well able to satisfy the questions and hesitations of a novice, kindly consented to bear me company. The William Pit mine was the scene of my adventure, the last opened and said to be the best planned work of its kind, and the most complete in all its conveniences of any in the kingdom. The shaft leading down to it is near the foot of the hill, which flanks the town to the east. Having equipped ourselves in dress suited to the dirtiness of our expedition, we repaired to the spot, and I took a peep into the black and bottomless hole without shrinking from my determination to go down. The coals are drawn up in baskets, 13cwt at a time, by the power of steam. The shaft is divided into three parts, one for ejection of water, one for the operations of the engine and one for the basket. Preparatory to our descent, our guide, one of the stewards cried out, "Coming Down" to the people below, a warning which is also attended to by the man at the engine, who moderates it's speed when any one is about to descend.*

The voice was answered from the depths below by a strange, hollow, distant, but loud cry which rather thrilled through my marrow - but I had now advanced too far to retreat with honour. We fixed ourselves in the basket, standing with our hands grasping the chain the word was given and down we glided with a smooth and scarcely perceptible motion through a duct about six feet in diameter and wooded all round. I kept my eyes firmly fixed in the aperture above, which contracted as I fell till at a vast depth, I was obliged to look down as my head grew dizzy and small pieces of coal and drops of water struck with unpleasant force against my face. As we descended lower all became darkness the noise over our heads grew gradually more indistinct till it died away and a dreary silence ensued, broken only occasionally by the grating of the basket against the walls. At length, after a descent of five hundred and seventy-six feet, I heard the voices of men below me, and presently perceived two dim lights. These were at the "High Eye", formerley the bottom of the shaft, on a level with which is a great extent of workings. I asked no questions here - "steady the basket", cried our guide and in a moment we were again in utter darkness. In a quarter of a minute more I heard other voices below me - the basket stopped and we soon found ourselves on our feet at the bottom, six hundred and thirty feet from the light.

I could here distinguish nothing but a single candle, with the obscure form of a man by it - all round was pitch dark, not a ray of light reaching the bottom from the mouth of the shaft. Before we proceeded to explore the mine, we were recommended to remain quiet a little in order to collect ourselves and while we were thus striving to be composed my nerves were momentarily shocked by a combination and succession of strange noises among which the loud clank of the chain as the empty basket dashed to the ground was particularly offensive. I never saw the object, and had no notice of it's approach till it's infernal crash always came to make me jump out of myself. While we were conversing here on the possible accidents that might occur in ascending or descending in the basket, we were told of a poor woman who lately had an extraordinary escape. It was her business to attach the chain to the basket and while she was in the act of doing this her hand became somehow entangled and the man at the engine setting it in motion before the proper time she was pulled from the ground before she could extricate herself, and dragged up as she hung by one arm, to the top of the pit, with no injury but a slight laceration of her hand.*

I had not become quite reconciled to the clank of the chain when we were summoned to go on. From the foot of the shaft we proceeded through a very

* The Hooker

long passage cut through rock with the roof arched and like the sides faced with bricks in a similar manner, an enormously expensive precaution but absolutely necessary to prevent the falling down of loose fragments of stone. I cannot describe scientifically, or with any degree of clearness and certainty, all the methods of proceeding that I have been adopted in laying out these vast subterranean works, and indeed such an account is scarcely called for, as the mine no doubt very much resembles in it's general plan many others that have been often described. In it's present state, as far as I could ascertain as I groped my way through the darkness, it appeared in the meeting and crossing of it's numerous passages to resemble the streets of a city - and a city of no mean extent, for we sometimes walked for nearly half a mile without turning between wall of coal or rock. To the right and left of the long lanes are workings, hollow spaces, five yards wide and twenty deep, between each of which a solid column fifteen yards wide and twenty deep, is left for the support of the roof, so that only one third of a bed of coal is taken away. Mr. Pennant observed that these columns appeared to him to be stores for future fuel, but they are left standing merely from necessity, and no material portion of them could be removed without danger to the great superstructures which they tend to uphold.

The coals are dragged from the workings in baskets, one at a time, by horses and carried to a place of general rendezvous, where by means of a crane they are placed on to the trams, nine of which, bearing burdens of nearly six tons, are drawn by a single horse to the shaft. A tram is a square board supported by four very low wheels, and a horse drags nine of them

Crane in Rolleyroad

An underground crane for transferring corves, as described by Richard Ayton on his visit to William Pit in 1814.

with their full cargo along an iron railway without any apparent effort.

The ventilation of the mine in it's remotest corners is said to be as perfect as is necessary, though I confess that in some places I felt no little difficulty in breathing. The air is rarefied by heat from a large fire kept constantly burning, and the current directed to the various workings through conduits formed by boarded partitions placed about a foot distant from the walls. Doors are placed at intervals in the long passages, which stop the air in it's course and force it through the conduits in the workings to the right or left. A current of air circulating through a multiplicity of foul and heated passages and chambers, must necessarily become languid in it's motion and impure in it's quality as it gets remote from it's source; but though I had occasionally to complain of some obstruction in the freedom of my respiration, our guide declared that he never felt the slightest inconvenience. I am not however inclined to generalise on the authority of this person's perception of the agreeable or disagreeable for in the midst of every kind of abomination that could be offensive to the eyes, ears and nose of a man, he walked along as if he had no senses quite distinct from my own, with the most profound unconcern.

The sensations excited in me as I descended down the pit did not really subside, and I wandered about the mine with my mind very much upon the alert, and under an indistinct apprehension of some possible danger which gave intensity to my interest in every thing that I heard and saw. A dreariness pervaded the place which struck upon the heart - one felt as if beyond the bounds allotted to man or any living being, and transported to some hideous region unblest by every charm and adorns the habitable world. We traced our way through passage after passage in the blackest darkness, sometimes rendered more awful by a death-like silence, which was now and then broken by the banging of some distant door, or an explosion of gunpowder that peeled with a loud and long report through unseen recesses of the mine, and gave us some idea of it's vast extent. Occasionally a light appeared in the distance before us like a meteor through the gloom, accompanied by a loud rumbling noise, the cause of which was not explained to the eye till we were called upon to make way for a horse, which passed by with it's long line of baskets and driven by a young girl covered with filth, debased and profligate and uttering some low obscenity as she hurried by us. We were frequently interrupted in our march by the horses proceeding in this manner with their cargoes to the shaft, and always driven by girls all of the same description, ragged and beastly in their appearance and with a shameless indecency in their behaviour, which awe-struck as one was by the gloom and loneliness around one, had something quite frightful in it and gave the place the character of hell. All the people whom we had met with were distinguished by an extraordinary wretchedness; immoderate labour and anxious atmosphere had marked their countenances with the signs of disease and decay; they were mostly half naked, blackened all over with dirt, and altogether so miserably disfigured and abused, that they looked like a race fallen from the common rank of man and doomed as in a kind of purgatory, to wear away their lives in these dismal shades.

I was much affected at the sight of the first individual whom I saw in one of the workings. He was sitting on a heap of coals, pausing from his labour, at the extremity of a narrow cavern, as gloomy a prison as ever was beheld. When we approached him he looked up, and a showed countenance which might have been that from which Sterne drew his portrait of a captive. He was an old man, and had so added to the effects of age in his looks that it was truly pitiable to see so worn and wasted a creature still owning to hard labour the support of his cheerless life. He was naked down to his waist and exposed a body lean and emaciated: his hair was grey and his face deeply furrowed and seamed with lines made by streams of sweat that had trickled down his blackened skin - a figure expressive of more wretchedness and humiliation than I ever saw before in a human being. This man was considered a very fortunate person, for he had worked forty-two years in the mines and never met with an accident. Few of the miners had served a third of this time who could not show some marks of the dangers of their employment, either from the firing of hydrogen or the fall of fragments of rock or coal. The coal is sometimes so loose and shattery that it cannot be safely worked without more caution than is often practiced by the miners, who, if they escape all injury for one day, are apt to forget on another that there can be any danger.

One class of sufferers in the mine moved my compassion more than any other, a number of children who attend at the doors to open them when the horses pass through, and who in this duty are compelled to linger through their lives, in silence, solitude and darkness for sixpence a day, When I first came to one of these doors, I saw it open without perceiving by what means, till, looking behind it I beheld a miserable little wretch standing without light, silent and motionless and resembling in the abjectness of its condition some reptile peculiar to the place, rather than a human creature. On speaking to it I was touched with the patience and uncomplaining meekness with which it submitted to its horrible imprisonment, and the little sense that it had of the barbarity of its unnatural parents. Few of the children thus inhumanely sacrificed were more than eight years old, and several were considerably less and had barely strength sufficient to perform the office that was required from them. On their first introduction into the mine the poor little victims struggle and scream with terror at the darkness, but there are found people brutal enough to force them to compliance, and after a few trials they become tame and spiritless and yield to themselves up at least without noise and resistance to any cruel slavery that it pleases their masters to impose upon them. In the winter-time they never see day-light except on a Sunday for it has been discovered that they can serve for thirteen hours a day without perishing and they are pitilessly compelled to such a term of solitary confinement, with a little consideration for the injury that they suffer, as is felt for the hinges and pulleys of the doors at which they attend. As soon as they rise from their beds they descend down the pit and they are not relived from their prison till, exhausted with watching and fatigue they return to their beds again. Surely the savages who murder the children which they cannot support are merciful compared with those who devote them to a life like this.

After rambling about for nearly a hour through the mazes of the mine, occasionally meeting a passenger or visiting a labourer in his solitary cell we were conducted to a spacious apartment where our ears were saluted with the sound of many voices mingling together in noisy merriment. This was a place of rendezvous whither the baskets of coals were brought from the workings and fixed on the trams, and a party of men and girls had met together here, who were joining in a general expression of mirth that was strangely contrasted with their apparent misery of their condition, and the dreariness of the spot where they were assembled. There was an unusual quality of light in this chamber which showed it's black roof and walls, and shone upon the haggard faces and ruffian like figures of the people, who were roaring with laughter at a conversation which outraged all decency, and resembled, as it appeared to my imagination, a band of devils. Some coarse jokes levelled at myself and my companion which we did not think it prudent either to parry or return, drove us from this boisterous assembly, and we were soon hidden again in the silent and lonely depths of the mine.

Our guide now led us to a passage where, in a small stream of water that flowed through it, we heard some air bubbling up which he knew to be hydrogen: he applied a candle to it when it instantly took fire, burning with a clear bluish light in a flame not larger than that from a small lamp. It continued visible when we had receded to a considerable distance from it, and had very beautiful appearance, shining like a brilliant star in the darkness, and giving an effect of exceeding depth to the gloomy avenue before us. While we were gazing at it with the profoundest stillness around us, we were startled by a report as loud as a clap of thunder, proceeding from an explosion of gunpowder. On going to the spot from whence it came, we found men working a passage through a bed of rock, called, in the language of miners, a fault, a phenomenon too familiar in coal mines to require any comment from me. This part of the mine was very remote from the shaft and so imperfectly ventilated that the heat and stench in it were scarcely supportable.

Not far from this place our guide regarded me with a very big and significant look and produced all the effect that he intended on my mind when he informed me that I was walking under the sea, and had probably ships sailing over my head. Considering this as the most extraordinary situation that we had been in during our subterranean excursion, he pulled out a bottle of spirits from his pocket and drank our health's and a safe return to us with all due solemnity. This rite fulfilled we turned our steps towards the shaft, oppressed by the heat and foulness of the air, and anxious to see day. We had walked about four miles in various directions, but had explored half the mine even in it's lower part and had a labyrinth of excavations over our heads as numerous and extensive as those which we had been rambling and separated from them by a roof only nine fathoms thick. I was astonished to hear that the whole of this immense work was the hard labour of scarcely ten years - that the extensive space through which we had passed and the whole mine that we had left unexplored, were within this short period a solid body of coal and rock. The labour going on before our eyes appeared quite insignificant and imagination could scarcely conceive the formation by such means of this vast place, which struck one rather as some strange creation by the giant hands of nature.

We ascended to the higher works by a very steep path which, at an elevation of about sixty feet from the lower level, opens into the shaft. The miners figuratively call the shaft the eye of the mine and this inlet into the upper excavations is denominated the High Eye. It was here that our guide had given his warning of 'steady the basket' lest it should strike against the landing in it's descent. All the coals procured from the under workings were formerly dragged up to this point by horses, but the task was found so difficult and tedious that it was though expedient to sink the shaft to it's present level. From the edge of the landing place at the High Eye, I had a peep at the day through the opening which appeared at a dreadful height above my head, and contracted to a spot not bigger than the palm of my hand.

As we were not promised a sight of any novelty in the upper mine, we did not enter it but returned to the lower level one from whence we proceeded to the shaft of the James mine, through a long up-cast passage which in consequence of a late accident exhibits one of the most awful spectacles that can be be conceived. An unusual quantity of coals were taken from it, and it was thought necessary for the support of the roof to plant two rows of posts under it, which were composed of the trunks of the largest oaks that could be procured. They had not been fixed long when the roof began to sink, descending very slowly but with irresistible force, and bending or breaking every tree that stood beneath it. It did not sink much more than a foot, and people now pass fearlessly under it in the conviction that it has permanently settled. The passage however bears a very tremendous appearance, and I did not go through it without some agitation. The broken and splintered trees still remain and are such formidable mementoes of the insecurity of the roof that I involuntarily quickened my pace as I looked at them, lest I should hear the coals again cracking over my head. This part of our expedition was rendered exceedingly disagreeable by a sulphurous stream of water which flowed down the steep, casting forth an odour which touched even the nose of our guide. At the top of the passage are the stables belonging to the two mines, in which forty horses are kept and never see the light. The animals were all remarkably sleek and fat, seeming to suffer no degree of injury from the impurity of the air so pernicious to man. They have one advantage over fellow labourers of the nobler species, in being subject only to moderate work and this may be one of the causes of their superior plumpness and healthiness.

After leaving the stables I soon heard the clank of the basket chain in the James pit which called upon me to collect my resolution for the journey that awaited me before I could again be lodged in safety of the earth. This pit is not so deep, by a hundred and twenty feet, as that by which we descended and a faint circle of daylight appeared on the ground at the bottom, which sick as I was of the darkness, I thought very beautiful. The man at the engine having been warned that we were about to ascend, we again committed ourselves to the basket, and soon mounted aloft, gliding through the void so softly and silently that one might have imagined oneself under the wand of an enchanter. I watched the light with some anxiety as it strengthened upon the faces of my companions, till we reached the top where the bright sky, and the fields and the sea, and the busy crowd of people and all the cheerful bustle of life burst upon my view with an effect in the highest degree of exhilarating and delightful.

I had certainly been very much entertained in the mine and did not consider the annoyances that I endured, or the danger that I imagined as overbalancing the amusement of my visit to it. The time in the basket was a trial of the nerves not speedily to be forgotten, though a man should scarcely venture to talk of nerves on such an occasion for it is no uncommon thing for ladies to go down the pit, and I have not heard of any who behaved otherwise than with courage and patience. Accidents sometimes happen from the inveterate carelessness of the people who in their familiarity with danger lose all thought of caution. A few days before I descend the rope had broken while the empty basket was going down, not in consequence of any imperfection, that could be not be reasonably suspected but from having been worn out by long use. And yet there are people appointed to superintend all the machinery employed in the mines and see from time to time that it is trustworthy. The ropes used in these pits are flat and are much more durable than round ropes, being less apt to be cramped or cracked as they roll round the windlass. A rope will last for three or four years, and this durability it is that encourages the thoughtlessness of those whose observation they are trusted.

There are several passages into the mines by inclined planes, and six shafts; three at considerable distances from each other on each side of the town. The mines comprehend a connection of working from six to seven miles in extent east and west and from two to three miles on the transverse line. The whole of the town is undermined without the least danger as is supposed to it's security; and the workings extend under the harbour, and seven hundred yards under the sea. Six hundred people of various descriptions are employed underground and more than a hundred horses. I was surprised to see so few men labouring at the excavations till I learned the quantity of work that a single individual can perform. A man can separate five tons of coals in a day, and this is not considered as an extraordinary exertion. Twenty score of baskets, each basket containing 13 cwt of coals are drawn up from each of the six pits every day, which calculating six days in the week makes the annual quantity of coals separated from the mines amount to 486,720 tons.

In one's admiration of these vast results of industry and contrivance, one may spare a thought on the condition of the people employed, who are sunk into a state of the lowest wretchedness and wickedness. I have no disposition to indulge in any affection of fine feeling, or to signalise my philanthropy by any idle sentimentality about the ordinary hardships incident to the labouring classes. The wants of society make it unavoidable that some of us should suffer under disgusting and unwholesome occupations. We must have coals, and men must be found to dig them, in contempt of evils that embitter and shorten their lives. But if, in consideration of the general good of the community, it is not fit that we should regard partial misery with too keen a sensibility, it is not necessary that we should run into the opposite extreme, and view with total indifference the condition of those who are toiling and suffering for our advantage. The people in the mines are looked upon as mere machinery, of no worth or importance beyond their horse power. The strength of a man is required in excavating the workings, women can drive the horses, and children open the doors; and a child or a woman is sacrificed, where a man is not required, as a matter of economy, that makes not the smallest account of human life in it's calculations. In consequence of the employment of women in the mines, the most abominable profligacy prevails among the people. One should scarcely have supposed that there would be any temptations to sin in these gloomy and loathsome caverns, but they are made the scenes of the most bestial debauchery. If a man and woman meet in them, and are excited by passion at the moment, they indulge it, without pausing to enquire if it be father and daughter, or brother and sister, that are polluting themselves with incest. In recording this shocking fact, I speak from authority that is not to be doubted. Great God! and can nothing be done for the redemption of these wretched slaves? It is unavoidable, that they give up almost every blessing of life, they must sacrifice soul as well as body? These dismal dungeons are certainly not fit places for women and children, the removal of whom would be an act of humanity not dearly paid for, though it should wring a few pounds from the hard economy that rules their service. The estimation in which women are held is one test of the civilisation of a people; and it is somewhat scandalous, in a country of gallant men, to see them sacrificed to the rough drudgery of coal mines. If there were nothing but the filthiness of their occupation to complain of, it would be no extravagant refinement to feel that their sex should preserve them from it; it is not a little offensive to see them changed into devils in their appearance, but it is afflicting indeed to witness the perversion that takes place in their moral character. They lose every quality that is graceful in woman, and become a set of coarse, licentious wretches, scorning all kind of restraint and yielding themselves up with shameless audacity to the most detestable sensuality. Their abominations are confined during the day to the dark recess of the mines; but at night they are cast up from the pits like a pestilence to contaminate the town. We must have coals, as I have said, but we may have them through the intercession of a little humanity and liberality, without this lavish waste of morality.

I have already adverted to the hapless condition of the children confined underground, and I willingly say a word or two more on their behalf. Such an abuse of them is, without doubt, in the highest degree disgraceful to those who command their services and calls for execration from every mind that is open to any feelings of kindness and charity. We have lately raised a cry that will save thousands, in a distant country, from the pains and the ignominy of a miserable slavery, and should not behold with unconcern anything that bears the stamp of slavery at home. I am not comparing the injury done to these children to the widespread mischief of the slave trade, but they may both be referred to the same kind of cold-blooded tyranny; and a man torn from his country and his home and forced under the lash of a taskmaster, in a foreign land, has scarcely more reason to complain of injustice and cruelty than a child thus dragged from the light, from all natural joys in which childhood delights and buried in a dark solitude for thirteen hours a day. One might have imagined that in this country at least children might be committed to the care and protection of their parents without apprehending any material or extended abuse. But among people broken down by poverty, or brutalised by vice, the moral affections become cold and dull; and there are multitudes of wretches who, for bread or gin are ready to sell their children to any kind of misery. The victims immured in these mines prove the fact; and in further confirmation of it one might adduce the wretched little slaves of chimney sweepers, a numerous class of beings most infamously oppressed, whom it is not too serious to call a reproach to the country. The Law will not allow a man to starve his child or flog it to death, but he may cast it from his care with impunity and devote it to a servitude, that does cruel violence to it's nature - either sends it to an early grave, or if it lives, leaves it to struggle with the torments of an enfeebled constitution. Surely some legislative interference is required to restrain so barbarous and unwarrantable an exertion of power - to prevent the exposure of children to loathsome and unhealthy occupations, at least till they are of an age to give their consent. The cries of the little beings condemned to the mines have never, I imagine reached the ears of their noble proprietor; and if he should hear of their condition through my means, and secure their release, I shall have been accessory to an act of charity that I shall remember with pleasure through life.

I pursued my journey from Whitehaven alone, my friend's time being too valuable to him to permit him to make such frequent and long pauses as my more multifarious concerns made it necessary for me to do. On leaving this town my chief subject of attention was still the collieries, which give quite character to the county: for many miles to the northward the eye is caught by the vast chimneys of the steam engines sending forth clouds of black smoke; roads with black coal dust lead to the various towns which are planted on the coast; files of coal-wagons are continually passing and repassing, and almost every person that one meets, shows, in his black figure, that coals here make up the grand business of life. The county is exceedingly populous; four considerable towns accruing on the coast within an interval of ten or twelve miles, besides many villages and hamlets. The appearance of the coast, enlivened by this great show of human art and industry, is very striking as viewed at some distance from sea. It forms a very beautiful line, being broken into a series of small bays, in each of which stands a town, with it's harbour and a thick cluster of masts in front, and backed immediately by gentle and cultivated hills, behind which in the distance, appear the dark summits of the mountains.

So ends Ayton's account of the visit to Whitehaven. Parton, Moresby, Workington, Maryport are briefly described by Daniell as he continued the "Voyage" alone into Dumfries and Galloway.

REGULATIONS

IN THE

WHITEHAVEN COLLIERIES,

RELATIVE TO THE USE OF

Sir Humphrey Davy's Safety Lamp.

Notice is hereby given,

THAT if any Hewer, or other Workman, employed in the *Whitehaven Coal-Pits* where any Danger can exist from *Fire Damp,* shall neglect to approach his Work with the SAFETY LAMP, or shall use CANDLES in doing so, he shall (for every Offence) forfeit the Sum of *Five Shillings.*

And when Orders are given to continue the Use of the Lamp, *during the whole Time of Working,* any Person, who shall remove the SAFETY CYLINDER, or use CANDLES in the Workings, shall also forfeit *Five Shillings.*

From the repeated Accidents, which have happened, and more particularly in the MORNINGS, by Workmen going incautiously into their Workings, (and which, had the *Safety Lamp* been used as directed, would have been prevented,—the Danger discovered,—and the lamentable and melancholy Effects avoided,)—it is expected that all Considerate Workmen, setting a proper Value on their own Lives and the Lives of their Fellow-Labourers, will give immediate Information of any Neglect to comply with the above REGULATIONS. And the Person, or Persons, so informing, will be entitled to the THANKS of the AGENTS, and also to One Half of the Fine; the remaining Half to be appropriated to the Fund for the Sick Colliers and their Families.

N. B.—LAMPS are supplied *gratis,* at the Granary, to the Miners, on Condition of keeping them in Order, and to be returned when any Man leaves the Service.—Any Workman, going to Work with a *Lamp* in an imperfect and unsafe State, shall be fined *Five Shillings,* under the same Conditions of the other Fines before named.

The OVERMEN, of the respective Districts in the Collieries, are responsible for the Miners being *compelled* to use the Lamp, and not to use Candles, except in those Parts where it is ascertained that no Danger will be occasioned by removing the *Safety Cylinder,* or using *Candles,*—which will always depend upon the Situation and Nature of the Workings.

Colliery Office, Whitehaven, 13 Nov. 1819.

J. Ware, Printer, 26, King-street, Whitehaven.

Public Notice Concerning Safety Lamps

So successful were the trials of Sir Humphrey Davy's Safety Lamp in William Pit, that the device was soon adopted throughout the Whitehaven collieries. This notice was produced following the Kells Pit explosion of 30th October, 1819, in which 21 miners lost their lives as a result of one of them removing the 'Safety Cylinder' (gauze) from his lamp.

Chapter 9

Extracts from the Memoir of Joseph Hodgson

Joseph Hodgson was one of Whitehaven's best-known 'characters' and was generally known as "Putty Joe," since he styled himself 'Glazier' in many of the little publications he produced.

Born on Good Friday, 1810 at Charles Street, Whitehaven, Joe received very little schooling and lived in extreme poverty for most of his life. For many years he existed as an itinerant worker, travelling the length and breadth of Britain on foot, taking whatever jobs he could find. Whenever he found himself with a little money in hand, he supplemented his precarious existence by writing and having printed an extensive collection of pamphlets which he sold from the basket he always carried. His little leaflets generally sold at 1d or 2d, but he charged up to 6d. for his more ambitious works. His autobiography, "Memoir of Joseph Hodgson, Glazier, A Native of Whitehaven," was published around 1850 and sold at 4d. This remarkable booklet, written in his own inimitable style, gives an insight into living conditions amongst the poorest stratum of society in Victorian times, and deserves to be better known. His experiences as a miner at William Pit amply confirm the horrors described more fluently by Ayton. Very rarely does he give dates for the incidents described, but in most cases these can be deduced using other evidence. Occasionally his memory is flawed, but by and large, his reminiscences 'ring true'.

Hodgson's mother was widowed, with four children when he was two years old, and received "Parochial Assistance" (payments from the Poor Law Relief Fund). She also had three daughters by a previous marriage. The family "lived in a cellar at that time with two apartments" Nevertheless, she somehow managed to arrange a little schooling for young Joseph, and at Mr. Alsop's school he "learned to read and spell the first lessons in Markham's spelling-book, in one week." Sadly, his school-days were over shortly afterwards. The following abstracts are taken verbatim from his Memoir:

> *My school-boy days had not long to continue ....for my mother not being of ability to keep us at school, and at about this time, she having become acquainted with a man considerably younger than herself, they were ultimately married; and as he was a miner, he soon had my oldest brother and myself into William Pit, and we had five pence a day each for minding trap-doors. I got severely buffeted, whipt and kicked; and one morning,*

when I came home and had breakfast (he must have been working the night shift) *my mother was washing me, and seeing the ridge or mark of a whip-crack along the side of my face, remonstrated with my stepfather, then taking his breakfast, who being very excited, upset the table, breaking all the delf* (crockery) *and in his animal propensity or unnatural rage he said I should go no more; but my brother continued, and in the course of a few weeks after, the pit exploded with firedamp, and my brother Thomas, and one Peter Hine, were the last two got out with life. Fifteen were killed, and the major part of my unfortunate abusers met with an untimely exit......* (This explosion occurred on the 16th April, 1821; twelve, not fifteen, died.)

A short time after the catastrophe referred to, my step-father and mother were solicited by two under-ground stewards, to admit me back again; and I had once more to descend into the bowels of the earth, to obtain part of a living, with not even the use of an oil-lamp, so essential to a miner, but a half-penny candle some nights;.....The first night I was there, the rats ran away with my bread, or bait, as it is termed by the miners.

He "*continued some time*" at the pit, then was laid off, and worked in various of the town's rope or twine-walks for three pence a day. His mother was compelled to sell their furniture at public auction, and Joe and his step-father made an abortive trip to Newcastle in search of work. On their return, Joe worked for a fortnight peeling willows for a basket-maker at three half-pence per day. After that he gathered spilled coal from the waggon-ways and wood chippings from the shipyards to sell as fuel, but later he became a labourer in a plasterer's business at four pence a day. He, and William McCullock were discharged when work became short. McCullock proposed that they should seek work at William Pit :

.....I objected to it through no aversion to the pits, only I accompanied him the first night, and in the course of a few weeks the pit fired or exploded, when he, with thirty-one more human beings met with an untimely end, and eighteen horses were also killed.

Shortly after this disaster, which occurred on the 13th October, 1823, Joe again went to work at William Pit for a short time, then returned to work for the pasterer when business picked up. After two accidents whilst climbing high ladders, suffering serious injuries from the second, he was unable to work and was forced to "*remain whole nights in the stables, and sometimes got a few beans to masticate, to appease the calls of hunger, and allay the cravings of my gnawing stomach*". After he had recovered he returned to the pit once more :

.....In the course of a few weeks there was a memorable incident, I shall here relate. My brother Thomas was driving a horse there; the same day, the major part of the pit's crew were panic-struck with the horrid and awful report, that the pit was about to explode, and the forebodings and awful circumstances of our then situation, and the mere impossibility of escape was quickly told from one to another, with quivering tongues and distorted countenances, and almost palsied frames, amongst the most appalling and horrid apprehensions and human dread that is imaginable, fearing that we were about to be awfully mutilated, burned, killed and destroyed, and running and crowding the road towards the pit shaft in an almost frantic confusion.

For once, it proved to be a false alarm, but the incident serves to illustrate the constant state of tension under which the miners worked. Joe remained at the pit for a few days more, then took a series of badly paid jobs, plastering, loading coal into steam-ships, and helping to fetch stones for road-work by ship from Parton.

I worked about in this sort of way with various success for some time. I then procured work in the pit again, and officiated in various sorts of pit work.....

One Sabbath night, I was inadvertently toying, or playing with a crane, which is used in lifting baskets of coal from one tram or carriage to another, and had the first finger-end pinched off, and a thumb much lacerated; and another day, an empty tram passed over both my legs, tearing the flesh from the bone, and causing extreme pain, with other minor accidents. And also one I shall here mention, as it well nigh cost my life. I was driving a black horse called Sprightly, at the time, a good and tractable pit-horse, and riding on the tram-end quietly, between the horse and the basket, when the fore-wheels leapt over the rails, then the basket was up-set on my back, and being firmly pressed on the cammarels of the horse with my breast, prevented me from calling assistance.....but not being far from the coal hewers, four men immediately came to my assistance, and gathered me out from amongst the horse's legs......As soon as I had recovered from my dilemma, I walked towards the pit shaft; but when I ascended near to the surface, the pit exploded, and killed the four men that so recently saved me......

If this incident actually happened at William Pit, no other record of it appears to have survived. It is possible that it is a garbled account of an explosion at *Croft* Pit in 1828, when *five* men were killed; Hodgson makes no reference to having worked there.

Several other accidents during this period are described, including a roof-fall, and the following potentially devastating occurrence :

> *Soon afterwards, a fatal accident occurred, by the new engine furnace igniting or setting fire to the coal wall, and sending forth the smoke and sithe, which eventually caused the death of nine men. And I remained down in the pit that day driving water that was sent down the pit-shaft to extinguish the fire.*

This occurred on 2nd. January, 1826. Joe then left the pit for a time, but after several adventures in the north of the county, he returned to Whitehaven :

> *When returned I was almost destitute of every essential necessary to human life, until once more I was doomed to go to William-pit. I will here relate one or two fatal accidents that happened during my stay, one a loyal and esteemed companion of my youth, named James Murray, who lived at George's-pit. One day, I being done work, a little before him, and passing him on my way homewards, he desired that I would remain until he was done with his work, that we would go outwards together, but I omitted waiting, having a little hurry on myself, and I proceeded towards the stables, on my horse's back ......and I ascended the pit, and had not been above ten minutes at home when I heard of the fatal exit of my loyal companion, by jumping on a full basket of coals at the main band-eye, and missing his hold on the chain and falling fifty fathoms down to the low-bottom and having his legs and arms broken, and otherwise dreadfully mutilated. I ran on hearing it, with borrowed speed to the bank-top, and viewed for the last time the mutilated and awful remains of my loyal companion, James Murray; and when the cart took him away to his widowed mother, I felt a piercing bereavement at his loss.*

He then describes the death by drowning of one of the horses he was unyoking, of another which fell down the shaft at James Pit, and the amazing survival of Thompson Wear's terrier which also fell down a shaft, but landed in a basket of hay being wound to the top. Thompson Wear was later to lose his own life by falling down the shaft at *Saltom* Pit. Again, Hodgson is slightly incorrect; Wear died on 4th June, 1834, by falling down the shaft of *Croft* Pit.

Putty Joe's next 'escape' from mining was to sail as a hand on the "New Draper" under Captain Barwise. This vessel was one of the many collier brigs engaged in the coal trade to Dublin. Joe was badly equipped for such a voyage, being *"ill supplied with clothes, I only having one old jacket, with two pairs of old stockings* (one hopes he also had trousers and shoes!) *and a moderate bed, which presented on the whole a wretched equipment for the sea, at the approach of winter.*" He managed, somehow, and after returning to Whitehaven, joined the crew of the 'Betsey'. He stayed with her for nearly six months, after which he remained ashore. Betsey made one more round trip to Dublin, then set sail for America. She foundered with all hands; Joe had had another narrow escape from death.

After one more brief period of working as a miner at James Pit, he set off on a series of extraordinary journeys on foot which took him to most parts of Scotland and England, which were to occupy the next twenty years of his life. At last, however, he settled down permanently in his home town, and established his own small business as a glazier. He continued to produce his fascinating pamphlets, to lecture, read his poems and sing in local concerts; without doubt, this self-taught man was one of the most remarkable personalities ever born in the town of Whitehaven.

Chapter 10

The Colliers and Their Pay

The purchasing-power of a given monetary unit inevitably declines over any appreciable length of time. Furthermore, the rate of its devaluation seems to have become progressively faster over the centuries. For many decades the purchasing power of a particular denomination of coin might remain stable, only to fall rapidly as a consequence of war, famine or other factors. The cost of particular commodities, too, varied enormously in relation to each other. The price of butter, for example, remained fairly constant over a long period, whilst tea, drunk only by the most wealthy in the late 17th Century, was cheap enough, by early Victorian times, to be found in practically every household. The imposition of Customs and Excise Duties also has a considerable effect upon the cost of many commodities.

The price of beer is a useful indicator of devaluation. In Tudor times, a penny provided a soldier with his daily ration of two thirds of a gallon of beer, whilst the mid-Victorian penny would have paid for only a pint of the cheapest beer. Today's 'new' penny (although nearly two and a half times the value of the pre-decimalisation coin) buys little or nothing. In today's terms, the Tudor soldier's pennyworth of beer would cost over six pounds, and the Victorian pint around £1.20p.

Such fluctuations make direct wage-comparisons over a lengthy period meaningless. The average weekly wage of about ten shillings (fifty pence) received by an underground labourer at Whitehaven Colliery in 1802 represented a subsistence-level wage, whereas today it would barely buy half a dozen eggs. It must also be born in mind that a high proportion of the Lowthers' work-force received free housing and fuel, so that whilst their pay was somewhat less than those of miners at Workington or Newcastle, these perquisites ensured parity. If one employer were to offer substantially greater, or substantially less recompense for similar work, migration of labour would be certain to follow. This was why, in Newcastle, miners were 'bound' (compelled to sign a contract for a fixed term of work) whilst the Lowthers' workforce was induced to remain by the provision of 'tied' housing.

The labouring classes throughout Georgian and early Victorian England were generally paid little above mere subsistence-level wages, and many of them were little better-situated than the slaves in colonial plantations, being compelled to toil for inconceivably long hours in appalling, often extremely dangerous conditions. Indeed, common soldiers and sailors were flogged, beaten and abused sometimes even executed, in much the same manner as slaves. In practice the killing of a slave was rare;

a replacement might cost anything from £10 to £70 - a slave represented a capital investment by the owner. Not so the 'free' workman who died or absconded. The pool of available labour would soon provide a replacement. As the movement for the abolition of slavery eventually ended this inhuman practice, so in England, the Coal Mines Act of 1843 and the efforts of Lord Shaftesbury and others in Parliament gradually improved the lot of the country's poor.

Despite the difficulties of comparing monetary values of the early 19th Century with those of today, it is nevertheless interesting to examine the pay-roll of a Whitehaven Colliery in 1802. This was immediately before the sinking of William Pit, and lists the rates of pay for some 453 workers then employed. It should be noted that the wages of 'haggers' (the men who actually extracted coal at the working face) are not specified. These were 'piece-workers,' whose pay was linked to their output. According to the amount of their effort, and the productivity of the seam being worked, they received an average wage of fifteen shillings, which in favourable conditions could rise to eighteen shillings a week. It would appear from the list that the Agent and his three Viewers - men with very responsible positions - were badly paid. This was certainly not the case; the pay-roll includes their weekly payments, but *does not take into account* substantial quarterly payments, and a bonus paid according to the overall profits from the collieries. It is estimated that in 1806, two Whitehaven Viewers each received about £300 for the year - equivalent to the wages of perhaps six or seven haggers.

The Pay-roll of Howgill Colliery, 1802.

The following table, based on the weekly wages of some 453 employees, does not include two groups of workers - the trappers and the steel-mill operators. These were invariably children, as were most of the tram drivers, gin drivers and many of the waggoners who *are* listed. It seems reasonable to suppose that around twenty to thirty trappers and perhaps a similar number of steel mill operators would have been employed, bringing the total to around 500. The smaller pits then working in the Whingill Colliery would have employed considerably less than this, although the number was to rise dramatically with the completion of William Pit.

Managerial (See Note 1)					
Occupation	**No.**	***Weekly Wage***	***Occupation***	**No.**	***Weekly Wage***
Agent	1	12s	Viewer	3	8s to 10s

Workers Above Ground			**Underground Workers**		
Occupation	**No.**	***Weekly Wage***	***Occupation***	**No.**	***Weekly Wage***
Basket Maker	6	14/-	Farr[illegible]	1	Not given
Mason	2	12/-	Banksman	1	12/-
Smith	3	12/- to 15/-	Hagger	81	12/- to 18/-
Labourer	29	4/- to 10/-	Filler (all female)	19	5/2d to 10/-
Cart	4	5/-	Tram Driver	70	5/- to 5/6d
Saddler	1	9/6d	Hooker	8	5/7d to 7/-
Fireman	8	10/6d to 11/10d	Gin Driver	11	2/6d
Striker	1	8/-	Banker	8	10/- to 12/-
Pick sharper	4	8/-	Attending way	28	4/- to 8/-
Craner	5	11/6d	Bearmouth roader	7	3/6d to 4/
Waggoner	16	5/6d to 6/6d	Engineman	5	12/- to 14/-
Tracer	2	5/6d	Mason	3	13/-
Carpenter	4	17/7d	Carpenter	1	12/-
Slatepicker	20	3/- to 4/-	Labourer	22	7/- to 15/-
Stagewhipper (See Note 2)	5	15/-	Hagger labouring	2	10/-
Blasters at Kells Drift	3	20/-	Attending Fox Pit Fire	2	8/- to 10/-
Lame persons doing nothing	2	5/-	Drivers jobbing underground	3	5/-

Pit Top and Coal Transportation					
Occupation	**No.**	***Weekly Wage***	***Occupation***	**No.**	***Weekly Wage***
Groom	11	6/- to 11/-	Changer	2	1/9d
Granary Cart (See Note 3)	1	9/-	Gatewatcher	4	2/6d
Gin Driver	2	2/- to 4/-	Fireman	1	11/-
Waggoner	18	12/-	Filler	2	not given
Carpenters (waggonway)	4	12/6	Trimmer	9	12/-
Steathman (See Note 4)	1	8/-	Waggoners (with horses)	6	21s to 24s
Assistant Steathman	1	7/-			

NOTES:	
1) Managerial Staff:	In addition to their weekly wages, managerial staff received substantial quarterly salaries raising their total annual payments to approximately £120 for the Agent, and £100 for each of the Viewers
2) Stage whipper:	Pit-top overseer (at a later period there were also underground stagewhippers).
3)Granary cart:	The granary building, in addition to operating as a grain store was equipped with workshops, and served as a store for mining equipment; the cart was used to deliver goods and materials to the pits.
4)Steathman:	Man responsible for controlling the steathe (staithe) in which coal was stored ready for shipment.

Certain perquisites were available to the Whitehaven miners; the Lowthers established a large granary, which they filled with oats when prices were low, but when prices above the rate of five shillings for three Winchester Bushels, miners were allowed to buy this basic commodity at that fixed rate. Miners and their families usually had the benefit of free housing and fuel, whilst the dependants of miners who died whilst in the Lowther's service, or were killed or maimed in the course of their work, were allocated a free house and a small weekly payment. Basic medical attention was provided for the injured, and if necessary they were afterwards given light work such as normally done by women or children. Occasionally such duties were nominal - the above list refers to two "lame persons doing nothing," but who were nevertheless paid five shillings a week.

The Lowthers, then, may be regarded as reasonably enlightened employers by the standards of their times; after the 1839 disaster, Lord Lonsdale paid the funeral expenses, medical attention where necessary, and ensured that widows and their families continued to receive the benefit of free housing and coal. In addition, they received a pension of two shillings a week. His Lordship's collieries were yielding large profits, of course, but it must be born in mind that a substantial amount of these profits were 'ploughed back' each year by way of capital investment in the industry itself, and in land purchases necessary for future development.

An extract from Bateman's letter to Lord Lonsdale (12th December,1802) throws some light upon the profitability of the industry at that time :

> *I hope we shall now ship from Howgill and Whingill about 1350 waggons pr. week at 14/- is worth £945 & I expect we shall not want above 370£ weekly besides the amount of the Country sales* (local sales as opposed to export) *to pay the workmen, & suppose Materials average 175£ pr. week,*

which I hope will be too much (he was allowing a safety margin in this estimate) *these two sums make 545£ taken from 945£ leaves 400£ pr. wk or 5200£ pr. Quarter* (quarter-year) *for profit.*

However, extensive repairs were being carried out on the Saltom Pit engine, an extension to the waggon way at Kells was considered **"Absolutely Necessary"** and a similar extension was needed at Wilson Pit, where "*the roof of the old works is all coming together and it is very expensive and dangerous. I hope in a little time we shall get the works into a pleasant state again.*" The Lowthers were making very considerable profits from their pits, but they were constantly having to invest in maintenance and development work. Bateman's letter continues :

We want Haggers much, we could take on 20 or 30 more, the profit upon each Hagger until we have enough at 2 waggons per day is 14/- or £4-4s-0d pr. Week. Pray would it be right to advertise for colliers in the Newcastle, Manchester & Scotch papers for a few weeks. When we wanted men ***formerly*** *I used to give the Men belonging to these works a Gratuity for every Collier they brought if they stayed a week, I also used to give the Strangers same ready cash, this had a wonderful effect. I see no other method left now for Mr. Curwen has late-by given his men such increased privileges that I fear we shall not get many more of his men, the 4 good men of his who promised to come (& who I mentioned to your Lordship)* ***have never arrived.***

At the time, Bateman was negotiating a price increase of a shilling a waggon in Dublin. A footnote to this letter is revealing :

I hope we shall get the 15/- per waggon as I find some advances will be necessary amongst your Lordship's principal Workmen, Engine men, underground Carpenters, & Smiths; Mr. Curwen gives 3/- per shift, we have only given 2/- but I advanced them 6d. last week, & they are not yet satisfied, we must advance further or they will leave the works.

On the 7th of January 1803, Bateman reported further

....In obedience to your Lordship's orders we got a Warrant this morning for six of the Colliers gone back to Workington. We have made three of your people here special Constables & they will be at Workington about six o'clock this evening to try to take the Men in their own Houses.

Last week was one of the unpleasantest we ever experienced. Mr. Curwen's Agent (Cowey) came to the Newhouses & offered the Haggers

4/6 per day certain, if they could not make that sum at their price of Hagging Mr. Curwen would make it up to them. The women fillers of Coals he offered 12d. per score (above double our price) *or 14/- per week; all their Children above ....(No figure given) years of age to be trap door keepers, they would give in their Hand on arrival at Workington from one to five Guineas for each Hagger....*

What Mr. Curwen can mean by such conduct I cannot guess; he knows, I dare say that all your Lordship's people are hired Servants & that he cannot legally keep one of them....He must likewise know that with your Lordship's Permission & a few guineas I can take from him twice the number of men he has got at this place....I own I dislike such conduct very much because the Men all become Masters, more money is given for work than it deserves & they get Drunk with the overplus & behave themselves very ill....

Bateman knew perfectly well what Mr. Curwen meant by this practice, and was happy to repay in kind! In fact, the poaching of workers often involved more than simple bribery; on the 5th December of the same year, Bateman reported

We purpose going to Clifton Common in a few days....we will get I. Powe of Clifton (whose Father was Agent there) to meet us & hint to him that a colliery will very soon be opened there unless the Greysouthen new Colliery returned the men they Kidnapped from us by repeatedly sending Agents here to offer them an advance of wages. I think in future they will not get any Person to come for them, as our people gave **Pickering**, *their Agent a thrashing the last time he came....*

Bribery, threats and violence were employed in the constant battle for labour.

Another source of violence stemmed from the practice of paying the workforce by the fortnight rather than on a weekly basis. This no doubt created financial difficulties for the lowest-paid miners, but the problem was exacerbated by the fact that instead of being paid at their place of work, or at the colliery office, they were given their money in various public houses on Saturday evenings. This was an incredibly stupid practice, which inevitably led to trouble. On the 27th August, 1833, The Whitehaven Herald carried the following report :-

POLICE - We have before had occasion to notice the scenes of drunkenness and riot, arising from the indolent and pernicious custom adopted by the colliery stewards of the Earl of Lonsdale, of paying the

colliers fortnightly, and giving them money in gross, to be divided in public houses on Saturdays. The natural and usual consequence is a debauch, often of three or four days, in which the best-disposed men can scarcely avoid the temptation of joining, and which always lasts pretty far into the Sunday. Scarce a Saturday Night passes without some disgraceful outrage, or a Sunday morning in which the streets in the neighbourhood of the public houses, are not filled with inebriated colliers, staggering home or turning out to settle their disputes by a battle.

All this passes without scarce any interruption by the police, who very seldom venture to interfere. We rarely take the trouble of recording incidents of this description, as their commonness makes them a matter of course, but, on Sunday last, a riot occurred, so disgraceful that we should do wrong in passing it over. Between two and three o'clock in the afternoon, the market-place, and its neighbourhood, were all in an uproar, in consequence of a battle royal among the colliers, a large party of whom turned out of a neighbouring public house, drunk and half naked, for the purpose of fighting. The streets were at the time filled with persons going to different places of Worship, who succeeded in separating the combatants, before the tardy arrival of the Police. We suppose, as usual, no notice will be taken of the affair by the authorities, but we trust that this public notice of the fact may bring it to the knowledge of the Earl of Lonsdale, and induce him to interpose, to put a stop to a mode of payment so injurious to private morals and public decency.

The proprietors of the Herald were somewhat naive in supposing that their rebuke would immediately bring about a change in the arrangement for paying the colliers. Further reports of similar brawls appeared on the 5th November and on 21 January the following year.

On 2nd September 1843 the same newspaper featured a very informative article concerning colliers and their pay:-

THE WHITEHAVEN COLLIERS

In none of the Whitehaven pits are the colliers bound. They work by piece, being so much a basket for the coal they take up, the amount varying, of course, with the quality of the coal, its situation and the amount of labour expended upon it. They work on what days and at what hours they choose, but the length of time during which they remain underground does not always indicate the actual extent of their employment, as they work in relays, and many of them prefer to remain in the mine unoccupied, instead of going to their homes (which lie at a considerable distance from some of the pits), and returning to take their turn. We hardly need add, that they receive no pay whilst they are so unemployed. Like the weavers in some of the manufacturing towns, the colliers have what might be called "idle days," which are Mondays and Tuesdays, on which they generally work but little, if any, though as the work advances (like the weavers again) they "push" the harder, and, it is but reasonable to suppose, in many instances labour harder than it would be possible for them to do for six days together.

On entering the mine each collier is supplied with "gear", in the shape of picks, wedges, and hammers, which he has to buy. The cost ranges from £3 to £4, which he liquidates by a weekly installment, which is stopped from his wages. Taking the amount so stopped at 1s. per week and the cost of the gear at the minimum, thirteen months will elapse before he gets rid of this drawback upon his wages; but the amount stopped is often only sixpence a week, and in such cases does not press so heavily upon his earnings. The "gear" is renewed when worn out, or repaired when repairing is necessary, at the expense of the coal owner, and when he leaves the mine, the collier, on delivering it up, is paid to the extent of its value. But riddles and shovels, which are included in the gear, are repaired at the cost of the collier himself. The safety lamp, an indispensable article to the miner, and one that requires renewing from time to time, costs him 5s. He is at the expense, too, of powder for blasting coal, which costs him at least 6d. and oil, for lights, costing him at the outside, about 1s. a week. The cost of repairing his gear and of powder, amounting altogether about 10d. a week, is deducted from his wages by his employers; the oil he purchases himself from whom he pleases He subscribes if married 4d. and if single 2d., each month for medical attendance. These then, are, as far as we have been able to ascertain, the out-goings of each collier, amounting in all, exclusive of the original cost of "gear", to say at the utmost 2s.6d. a week or 5d. a day.

Now with regard to the wages of the colliers. We have before us the names and average weekly earnings during six weeks ending 12th August, of 147 men employed in the Croft, Wilson and Duke Pits. From these we find that the total number of days for which all the men have been paid is 4,139, which gives an average to each of 28 days, and a fraction which we omit. The total sum of money earned by them during the same period was £687.3s.7d, the average of which is £4.13s.5d. Having worked, on the average, 28 days each, their average daily earnings must have been somewhere about 3s 4d.

It must, however, be borne in mind that from this sum is to be deducted the "drawbacks" which we have specified above, amounting to some 5d. a day, and the "Off-takings" to which we have not yet alluded, for "slack" baskets (baskets not properly filled) and baskets containing "small" and "splint". These vary in amount, according to the size of the basket and the quality of the coal, and run from three-pence to ten-pence. In the Duke Pit, off-takings have been the greatest; of 12,084 baskets of coal raised by 56 men, 119 were rejected for some of the faults specified; about one and a half in every hundred, or stating it differently, the 56 men have each been stopped nearly two baskets in six weeks. The average of each of the other pits does not vary materially from that of the Duke Pit. In the three, during the six weeks referred to, 28,120 baskets of coal have been raised by 176 men, and of these 273 have been rejected. It should be stated that the miners live in rent-free cottages, receive 6d. a week in addition to the wages they earn, to purchase coal, and when "maimed" by accident, are allowed 5s. a week during their illness.

We now have stated the facts as they have come to our knowledge relative to the mode of employment and the amount of earnings of the colliers in the three pits, which we can see no reason to doubt form a fair criterion for the rest. If we have fallen into error, we shall cheerfully rectify it when it is pointed out.

On 12th December 1882 a letter relating to miner's pay was published in the Whitehaven Gazette. It was written under the *nom de plume* X.Y.Z. This, almost certainly, was Joseph W. Wallace, one-time editor of a Manx newspaper and the founder and proprietor of The Cumberland Museum situated at Distington. Of a waspish disposition, Wallace was the author of a number of cantankerous letters on various topics to the local press, and this letter is in keeping with his style:-

WILLIAM PIT COAL HEWERS

Sir,- a notice was posted up at the William Pit top last Friday, stating that coal hewers would receive an advance of one penny per ton, to commence on the 11th inst. This speaks highly of the liberality of the colliery managers, when one considers the high wages these hewers were receiving previous. At William Pit, two men put out from twenty to twenty-five tubs per day, each tub weighing from twelve to thirteen cwt., that is, from*

* *20 cwt. (hundredweight) = one ton*

twelve to fourteen tons per day, at 1s 7d. per ton, showing each man can earn from 10s. to 11s. per day, which is nearly as high wages as when in 1872 and 1873 coal stood at such a high figure on the market. In Henry Pit the wages exceeds the William Pit a little, for although the tubs are smaller, the men put out an extra number, the average number of tubs per day being between thirty-five and forty.

Now, Sir, these colliers were never connected at any time with the Union, yet today they are in a better position than those of Northumberland or Durham, the great centres of unionism, as their wages exceed, in fact doubles the wages of any hewers in the northern district.

This speaks loud in favour of the Whitehaven Collieries, and all who see this will conclude the men have nothing to complain of; and it would be well if these men would in these prosperous times, put by, as the saying is "for a rainy day," which is the advice of - Yours etc., X.Y.Z.

The following week's Gazette contained a brief reply by one of the miners, who signed himself, appropriately "William Pit" :-

Sir, - As a hewer working in William Pit, I beg leave, with your permission, to give an emphatic contradiction to the letter which appeared in your paper last week, as I can scarcely keep soul and body together.

Undaunted by this reply, X.Y.Z. responded :-

Sir, - I saw a letter in your last week's issue giving an emphatic contradiction to the statements I made in your impression of the 16th. Inst., from a coal hewer residing in Mount Pleasant. In his letter he states "he can scarcely keep soul and body together." From enquiry, I learn this hewer is no criterion, because he is one of the many who can afford to drink three days of the week, commencing to work about Thursday, thereby scarcely working half time, whereas if he were to work an average number of days per fortnight, he would have been able to have provided a goose this Christmas, as I have been informed that into nearly two-thirds of the colliery houses a goose found its way, accompanied by either a quarter cask or half a barrel of ale. I have heard the saying "That poverty to some is a blessing;" and I think if the colliery officials had only posted up at their pit banks one penny or twopence per ton reduction it would have been better, as their liberality has been sadly abused this Christmas time, as the high wages have enabled men to exercise an extravagance which fully substantiates my former statements, notwithstanding the tame contradiction of this savant belonging to Mount Pleasant; and since his letter appeared I am able to give evidence of one of the hewers who some time since, went to seek his fortune in America, and has since returned and is now working in William Pit. He says he gets more money for less output by nearly double, and William Pit hewers are lords compared with the miners of Pennsylvania.

I need add no more after this testimony to prove that if this hewer living at Mount Pleasant would only attend to his work, he would have less time to find fault with his position, his work, or his employers ....

Whilst there may have been some truth in X.Y.Z's. scathing remarks, his references to membership of the Union were distinctly 'below the belt.' The Cumberland Miners Association had been founded in 1868, but Whitehaven miners were understandably reluctant to join. There was marked discrimination against union members who applied for work in the Whitehaven Pits, and miners who joined were dismissed from their 'tied' housing in the event of a union-inspired strike. This was serious enough in the case of a single person, but if he were married, with a family, the results would be catastrophic.

A Board of Trade report in 1886 stated that coal hewers in Cumberland averaged 24s.8d for their 48 hour week. Different rates of pay were made to miners in different pits within the same colliery, and hewers working thinner seams were paid slightly more per ton than those working in the Main Band. Wellington was by this time the biggest and most productive of the Whitehaven pits, employing considerably more workers than William, and paying them marginally better; the increase of 1d. a ton at William reduced this disparity a little, and helped to redress a very severe reduction in wages which had occurred some years previously. In March 1874, the wages of Cumberland's colliers had been reduced by 10%, with a further cut of 15% a few weeks later. In December of the same year a further 10% reduction was announced, at which point a strike was called. Union representation at Whitehaven being so small, the Lonsdale collieries remained open; but the 10% reduction was imposed throughout the coalfield. In this way, miners had lost more than a third of their income in less than a year. In November 1875 the coal owners called for a yet another 10% reduction in wages. After arbitration some classes of underground workers were forced to accept the whole 10% cut, others only 5%. Three strikes occurred in 1876 when colliers pay was reduced still further.

These severe cuts were not imposed by the coal owners simply to increase their profits; the Cumberland coal trade was seriously depressed at that time, unable to compete with coal from Scotland and Lancashire which by this time had secured over 80% of the Irish market. In 1879, a new method of determining wages was introduced. Each quarter-year, wages would be adjusted according to a 'sliding scale' based on the selling-price of the coal produced. This system, which was moderately successful, came to an end in 1889, when it was replaced by a Board of Conciliation which negotiated rates of pay.

In 1888, the Lowthers leased their Whitehaven collieries to Bain & Co., and sold their last remaining coal rights nine years later. After 250 years, the family ceased to hold any direct interest in Mining. As Bain and Co. took charge of the pits, Whitehaven membership of the Union increased rapidly. Strikes over pay and conditions of work occurred from time to time, culminating in a National strike which brought the industry to a standstill for five weeks in 1912. This was a crippling blow to Bains & Co. Already over-stretched financially by such developments as the new haulage plane at William, they were forced to relinquish their lease in the following year.

Chapter 11

The Oldest Working Miners

Before retirement at the age of sixty-five became compulsory in British collieries, each coalfield could boast of miners who were still working in their 70's and 80's. Indeed, there was strong rivalry between the coal-mining areas as to which employed the oldest, or the longest-serving collier. Whitehaven certainly had its fair share of such claims, of which the best documented are as follows :-

ALEXANDER HENDERSON

Alexander Henderson, or "Elick" as he was better known, first saw light on March lst, 1829, in a cottage at Sandwith, within sight of Wilson Pit. He was one of a family of seven boys and five girls born to Edward and Eleanor Henderson. Work was more important than education in those days, and Elick, like most children, went to work at an age when most children today are being transferred from Infant to Junior School. At Sandwith he attended a 'Dame School' known as Cabbage Hall, which was kept by an old woman. Then for a very short time he went to the village school, which had been built by subscription, aided by a grant from the National Society.

Elick's schooldays were short-lived, for at the age of seven he went to Croft Pit to help his mother pick slate from the coals at the *Pitbank* (later to be called the *screens*) At the age of ten Elick was given a job as a Trapper at sixpence a day (two and a half new pence). He started work at six in the morning, and finished at six and sometimes seven at night. At this time women worked down Croft Pit driving the horses. As Elick recalled there were about six of them and the horses they drove were big, strong and 'stiff built', unlike some of the pit ponies that were used in the small roadways.

After two years of trapping, Elick became a driver being paid a shilling (5 new pence) a day and by the time he was sixteen he was hewing coal at the coal face. Elick could remember when they used straws instead of safety fuzes for blasting the coal. "*We would get the straws from the farmers at harvest time and fill them with powder at home. To keep them from being damaged they would be carried into the pit in a hollow walking stick. If we were blasting coal the straws would be six inches long and a great deal longer in stone.*" He could also recall the dangers associated with the blasting. After boring the hole it was filled with a quantity of powder, then a nudle (a thin metal rod) was inserted before tamping in soft clay to seal the hole, the nudle was then withdrawn and the straw inserted. The straw would then be ignited by 'match paper', a type of brown paper saturated with a solution of saltpetre. The person responsible for lighting the match paper would light it and dash for cover. This method was used until the introduction of Safety Fuze in the 1850s. Elick worked at the face for about five years. The pit was 'ridden' (the men lowered in a basket down the shaft) at four in the morning and work continued until six at night; during the winter they saw sunlight only at the week-end.

At this period the coal at Croft and neighbouring pits was still transported in baskets and baskets were still used to carry workers up and down the shaft It was also a time when Davy lamps were in use but unlocked. The miners took them home to fill, trim and clean, but when the gauze became too dirty some miners would cut a hole in the gauze to give a better light. This practice was, of course, totally forbidden since any damage to the gauze rendered the lamp unsafe and could result in an explosion of gas. During Elick's time at Croft there were four explosions killing a total of fourteen miners.

Elick had a wonderful memory for incidents and detail. He recalled the time when an explosion ripped through the Duke Pit in 1844, killing eleven miners and ten horses. It would have been a bigger disaster, but on that same day many of the miners from Duke Pit were absent, attending the funeral of two youths who had been killed by falling out of the basket at Croft Pit.

Regarding the basket accident at Croft, Elick had good reason to remember that day. It was Tuesday the 9th January 1844, and he had ridden in the basket before the accident. He remembered that the basket had contained ten people, when it started its descend. When it had reached a depth of about thirty feet the rope slipped off the pulley and two youths named Daniel Lennon (21), and Christopher Kitchen (16), fell to their deaths. At the inquest, it was found that they had been standing on the edge of the basket and hanging on to the chains. He remembered that when women worked down Croft, it was *they* who would stand on the edge of the basket.

Elick became Overman then Under Manager and finally Manager of Croft Pit. In his later years he had the responsibility of superintending the aircourse of Croft Pit, a task which involved daily walks of inspection of from eight to ten miles. He was still performing this duty until shortly before his death on 15th April 1911 at the age of 82.

GEORGE STEPHENSON

The Guinness Book of Records, lists George Stephenson as "The most durable coal miner," having worked for 82 Years at William Pit. As we shall see, this claim is not sustainable.

He was born at Parton on the 21st April 1833, the eldest of a family of four boys and three girls. As a contractor, George's father kept several horses, and his eldest boy soon became useful to him. As soon as he was able, he began to assist his father bringing coal from Lamb Hill Pit, (situated on the East side of the 'Long Mile' opposite Parton Estate.) He worked with his father until he was 24 years old, when he decided to work as a collier at William Pit about the year 1857.

Until 1872, at William Pit, they were paid 10d a basket for coal, and later ls a basket. A William Pit basket held 11 cwt. A full six-day week of work paid them, in favourable conditions, an average of only 30s a week though in practice they were paid fortnightly. When the pay of all the pits coincided on the same day, that was known in the town as "the big pay day". When the workers of only some of the pits were paid, it was "the little pay day." The "Butty" would go to the pit to collect the wages, and the colliers would be told at what public house they were to meet for the "share out". That often resulted with the pay being lot lighter by the time it was got home! There was a method of payment in Stephenson's younger days when colliers' widows had the privilege of paying so many shift men at their houses, the widow having a commission of a penny in the pound or part of a pound on all sums they paid out.

Miners' Soup Kitchen 1912

In times of crisis, strikes, disasters or pit closures, voluntary groups quickly formed to mitigate the most serious effects. The notice pinned to the table reads "Support Whitehaven Miners Children. Provisions preferred."

Stephenson was never involved in any explosions, but was injured in a roof fall when his right forearm was so badly damaged, that it was thought it would have to be amputated. He told Dr. Robert Lumb, the colliery doctor, that his father had lost a leg and his brother an arm in accidents and he was not going to lose his arm. Luckily he recovered and continued hagging coals for thirty years after the accident. Then, at the age of 68 he was given a light job as a stable man underground for two years. Two years later he was deemed too old for underground work, and was then given a light job on the pit top where he remained until his retirement at the age of 89, in April 1922.

On his retirement, Mr. R. Steele, the works manager of the Whitehaven Colliery Co., presented George with a Treasury Note Case, containing 52 guineas. George Stephenson died on the 18th March 1926, a few weeks short of his 93rd birthday.

The above details of George Stephenson's life, were taken from an interview he gave to the Whitehaven News in January 1920. Clearly he was involved in colliery work for much of his long life, but the claim that he was Britain's 'Most Durable Miner' cannot be upheld. According to his interview, he did not start at William Pit until he was 24 years old. He was given a light job on the pit top when he was seventy. That would give him *underground* service of 46 years. He cannot be regarded as a miner during the remaining nineteen years he served at the pit top, where he would be classed merely as a surface worker. Alexander Henderson and William Cowan, whose coal mining careers are told in this chapter, had much more underground service than Stephenson.

The Sinking of Haig Pit, 1914

The sinking of Whitehaven's last shaft mine occupied most of period of the First World War, and, until its closure in 1986, it was the last operating in the Cumbrian coalfield. Only the Solway Colliery at Workington was sunk after Haig, in 1937, and it was to close sooner, in 1973.

WILLIAM COWAN

Sixty seven years continuous service in the Whitehaven pits, all of it underground! This was the remarkable record of William Cowan, who at the age of 81 was still merry and light hearted, and regularly enjoyed a hearty crack whenever he was visited by Dr. C. J. J. Harris. Apart from being his own doctor an old friend of the family, Harris was the official surgeon to the Whitehaven pits.

The son of an old Whitehaven miner, William Cowan was Baptised at Holy Trinity Church on 13th October 1844. He was the second oldest of eight boys, all of whom were to be employed in Wellington Pit. William started work at the age of eight, carrying lamps for the miners. In those days they used the original "Davy" lamps-with gauze all the way down. These gave a dim flickering light, but miners became accustomed to the feeble glow and were able to see surprisingly well. He also helped to look after the horses which pulled the tubs to the shaft. They were quite big horses, not at all like the usual pit ponies.

When he was eighteen he started hewing coal. He remembered the big fire in Wellington Pit in 1863. He was down the pit when it happened, and every one had to leave. No lives were lost but the pit was closed for a long time and the workers transferred to William and Croft Pits. At the time Mr. Burns was the manager of the pits and his foreman was John Armstrong. He did not remember women and girls employed underground, but recalled his father talking about them. All the women who

William Pit, 1939

This view from the seaward side shows waggons waiting to be loaded in the pit's marshalling yard, with the main railway line in the foreground.

were employed at the pit when he was young worked on the screens.

He married his wife Elisabeth when he was 26, and they went to live at 35, Front Row, Newhouses, where he lived for almost 60 years. His wife died on the 13th March 1913. William retired from pit work in 1920 aged 76, he passed away on the 2nd August, 1929. He is buried with his wife and son John in the old part of Whitehaven Cemetery. The grave is marked with a headstone.

The tragic death of their son John was reported in the local press. Young John was employed as a haulage hand in Henry Pit, later to become the downcast shaft for William Pit. How the lad came to be injured was never confirmed but he was run over by several waggons, and had both legs severely crushed. He was got out of the pit and taken to his home (not the hospital) which was the normal practice in those days. Dr Harris arrived at the house almost immediately, and deemed it necessary to amputate one of the lad's legs. This was done in the family home and young John died shortly afterwards; the date was 10th. November 1887. He was 13 years old.

The Cowan family were destined to suffer further tragedy. Margaret Cowan, the great-grand-daughter of William Cowan, was to lose her husband Patrick Murtagh aged 28, in the William Pit explosion of 1947.

The Laboratory at Haig Pit

After leasing the Whitehaven Collieries in 1933. Priestman Collieries built this laboratory to improve safety measures and quality control.

MICHAEL MORGAN

Michael Morgan was probably the oldest miner ever to have worked in the Whitehaven pits. Sadly, unlike Henderson, Stephenson and Cowan, he was never interviewed by reporters for the local press. The only record of him having worked in the coal mines is given at the inquest into his death which was published in the Cumberland Pacquet, Tuesday 22nd November 1853, as follows:

> *"An inquest touching the death of Michael Morgan, which had been opened by William Lumb Esq., on Wednesday, and adjourned to afford the coroner time to communicate with the Home Secretary, the cause of death coming within the class of colliery accidents, was brought to a termination yesterday evening. The facts of the case were few and brief. The deceased who was 86 years of age, was descending the shaft of William Pit in a basket by himself on Wednesday morning. He accomplished the greater portion of the descent in safety, but when within as is supposed, about 60 feet of the bottom, he was by some means thrown out of the basket, and on being picked up at the bottom was quite lifeless. The accident, in the opinion of Mr. Sawyers, was caused by the basket coming into contact with the "eye" of the pit, which was within ten fathoms of the bottom. He supposed deceased to have been looking out for the "eye" but on the wrong side, and when he was within a less distance than he was aware of; and probably to save himself caused the basket to come in contact with by placing against the side of the shaft the stick which, like all colliers, he carried to guide the basket in its descent. The bottom of the basket being intercepted by the "eye" it would tilt over, and the deceased would be thrown out. Mr. Sawyers stated that, in consequence of the coroner's communication to the Home Office, a government inspector had come down, and viewed the shaft, and said that no precaution against accident could be more complete than those adopted there. In allusion to the age of the deceased, which was stated to be 86 years, Mr. Sawyers stated that he might have ceased from work altogether, and would have received, according to their regulations, a retiring allowance of 4s per week, but as he could still earn 12s 10d weekly he preferred to work. It was at his own earnest request that the banksman allowed him to descend alone, as he wished to get the start of the other men of his gang in consequence of having to traverse a very steep ascent of about a mile in length below, to James Pit, in a very heated atmosphere, the air passing through about ten miles of chambers before reaching the place in question. The steep ascent was trying to the old man's strength which made him anxious to commence it before the arrival of the other men, to enable him to complete in the*

proper time. An order has since been issued, however, prohibiting any person being allowed to descend alone. The verdict of Accidental Death was returned."

The Last Tubs Raised from Haig Pit, 1982

Production from Haig did not cease until 1986, but for the last four years cages for raising coal in tubs were replaced by 'skips'.

Chapter 12

William Pit - The Final Years

Despite the very considerable improvements accomplished by the early investments of Bain and Co., output from the Whitehaven Collieries began to decline in 1909. The situation was aggravated by the costly National Strike of 1912, which brought all British pits to a standstill for five weeks. By this time several of the company's leading figures had died or retired, and in the following year Bain and Co. relinquished their lease and a new company, The Whitehaven Colliery Co. Ltd., took over.

The new lessees soon embarked upon their major undertaking, the sinking of Haig Pit between 1914 and 1918. This was destined to be come the last shaft-mine operating in the Cumbrian coal field. However, they, too, were to experience occasional strikes and geological problems which led to their downfall. In 1928 a fire occurred in the Main Band workings of William Pit, which had to be sealed off for some years. Thereafter, the less productive Bannock Band had to be worked instead. A series of small explosions cost a number of lives, and certain areas were becoming worked out. In order to reduce costs Ladysmith Pit was closed in December, 1931, and Wellington Pit in the following year, but it was becoming clear that the Company was in serious financial difficulties.

In 1933 Lord Lonsdale served a writ, re-possessing his leased pits. The two which were still operating in Whitehaven, William and Haig, were quickly re-let to Priestman Collieries, based at Newcastle-upon-Tyne. Again the new company at once invested heavily to improve working conditions and working practices in an attempt to improve efficiency. Further costly improvements were made to Haig's ventilation system, and to improve "quality control" an analytical laboratory was set up and a completely new screening plant was installed at William. The Haig screens were also extended and improved.

In 1935 the news that Priestman Collieries (Whitehaven) Ltd. was to enter into voluntary liquidation after only two years of operation, was greeted with horrified disbelief by the 2,500 employees, who had striven to achieve a doubling of the output for their new employers. Their efforts had been largely frustrated by geological problems; the gamble had failed. Once these miners were laid off, unemployment in Whitehaven reached 4,500, a rate of over 57% - one of the worst ever recorded in England. It should be noted, however, that two other large pits in the area, Walkmill at Moresby, and Lowca No. 10 were by this time owned by the United Steel Company, and continued in production throughout this troubled period.

For almost eighteen months Whitehaven's pits remained closed and no maintenance work was carried out, but in 1937 yet another company, the Cumberland Coal Co. (Whitehaven) negotiated a lease from the Lowther Estates. This new concern was Scottish-based, the controlling interest being held by the Coltness Iron Co. Ltd. of Glasgow. Mining operations were quickly resumed, and further improvements undertaken. Still more work was done on the air-ways, and a centralised power-house was set up at Haig to supply electricity, steam and compressed air wherever these were needed in the workings. Pit-head baths were introduced at Haig, but not at William. It was evident that future developments were to be concentrated at Haig rather than at the much older pit.

This policy proved justified as further setbacks occurred at William Pit. The explosion on the 3rd. June 1941resulted not only in the loss of lives, but in sealing off the two most productive seams, the Main and Bannock Band as a precaution against spontaneous combustion. This left the relatively small Six Quarters Seam as the only one still worked in the pit. At this time the outlook for any long-term production planning was decidedly bleak, and worse was to come with the major disaster of 1947, and the construction of a new Drift connecting Lowca No 10 Pit with the Six Quarter Seam in William Pit.

1947 was also the year in which Britain's coal mines were Nationalised, and the newly-formed National Coal Board quickly produced a scheme of re-organisation of Cumberland's Pits. This involved new methods of mechanised mining and larger scale operations. The future seemed secure for the Solway Colliery at Workington, and for Haig at Whitehaven, with its access to three highly productive seams, but it was clear that William Pit's days were numbered, along with many smaller pits in the county.

Although mining was resumed at William Pit in 1948, it was announced in September 1953 that the old pit was to close. The proposal was accepted by the workforce, and by the Cumberland Miners' Union, whose General Secretary, Tom Stephenson stated that:

> *The National Union of Mineworkers agrees that the coal can be got from No 10 Pit on a more economical basis than can be worked in William Pit, and the NCB proposal has our blessing. We have an assurance that there will be no redundancy. The 375 men employed at William Pit will be gradually transferred to Harrington No 10 and some to Haig.*

It was stated at the time that William Pit was then producing 1,200 tons of coal per five day week.

The editorial column of Whitehaven News, 17th September, 1953 expressed no regrets about the forthcoming closure :

> *The National Coal Board's decision to close William Pit, Whitehaven, by the end of 1954 did not come as a surprise; the closure has been indicated for some time as part of the reorganisation scheme. That such a step is advisable has been borne out by the fact that no objection has been raised by the miners themselves. They have been assured that every man employed at William Pit we be found alternative employment at Haig or Harrington and that suffices them. There will be no regrets about the passing of William Pit, not even on sentimental grounds. That terrible disaster of 1947, when 104 men lost their lives, is still fresh in our memory. During the last war an explosion cost twelve lives and an underground fire necessitated the sealing off of valuable workings.*
>
> *At least William Pit, after 1954, will not be able to take toll of the lives of Cumberland miners.*

The last tub of coal was raised through William Pit shaft on New Year's Eve, December 31st 1954. All the men and women ("screen lasses") were transferred to other pits, but a salvage team remained until its final closure in 1955. After 150 years "The most dangerous Pit in the Kingdom" became part of history.

A *Driver with his Rolley of Two Corves*

This naive illustration appeared in "The Whitehaven Miners Gazette and Public Advertiser", a monthly magazine which appeared during the 1920's. It shows a horse-driver taking two corves along the rolley road. Note the Davy lamp suspended from his belt.

Chapter 13

THE WILLIAM PIT DISASTERS

The most feared and dreaded sound in any mining community was the warning signal from the pit's steam horn, blasting out its mournful signal of one long followed by six short blasts, repeated over and over again. This was the signal used to inform miners and rescue workers that they had to report to the pit because a severe accident or explosion had taken place. This sound would be heard time and time again throughout Whitehaven's sorrowful coal mining years. No fewer than one hundred explosions of firedamp would take place before the final one in 1947. William Pit alone exploded at least fourteen times during its 150 year history, killing more than 200 men, women, boys, and girls. A further 100 would die from accidents in the pit.

An explosion can, in an instant, decimate a whole generation of menfolk in a mining community. On the 14th of October 1913, 439 miners were killed by an explosion of firedamp in the Universal Pit, Senghenydd Glamorgan, South Wales, the biggest ever such disaster in Great Britain. Whitehaven suffered its worst disaster on the 11th of May 1910, when 136 miners died in the Wellington Pit, the result of an explosion of firedamp, followed by a fire. At the lowest estimate, it is clear that more than 500 men, women, and children, lost their lives in the coal mines in the Whitehaven District from explosions of firedamp, and as many again from accidents, many of which were never reported.

The scenes at the pit top after an explosion were pitiful to observe. The women waiting for the bodies to be brought to the surface, then the inspection of each corpse to establish its identity; the horses and carts standing ready to convey the bodies to their respective homes; the heart-rending sight of the wife or mother with her shawl wrapped around her head, following the cart with the body or bodies of her menfolk covered with straw; the wailing of the supporting relatives and friends, as the sorrowful convoy of carts made their way through the town to the Newhouses where so many of the miners lived.

Some of these bodies were in a dreadful condition; an explosion of firedamp gives no quarter to anything in its destructive path - a husband, son or daughter, who had left home a few hours earlier might be returned as a severely charred or mutilated corpse. But if death had been caused by the afterdamp, the body might be unblemished, the victims appearing simply to have died in their sleep.

Because of the condition of the bodies they were usually buried the following day, normally in coffins supplied free of charge by Lord Lonsdale's carpenters at the Granary Yard. Before a victim could be buried, an inquest had to be held in order to ascertain the cause of death. Prior to the Inquest, the Coroner and Jury would visit each house in turn and examine the bodies, regardless of their condition. In 1831 after the Croft Pit explosion, a jury reported that *"Arthur McQueen and his nine year old son were lying in the same bed, very much burned"*.

The death of a 15 year old boy in December 1900, resulted with the body being handed over to the parents in a bag. Such was the terrible condition of the body, that the Jury protested to the Coroner for having been compelled to view such a sight as they had just seen. They thought that something should be done to alter the law in that respect. They were told that until the law was changed, there was no alternative but to view the bodies irrespective of their condition.

We make no apology for the sometimes harrowing descriptions of the aftermath of disasters at William Pit which follow. These tragic events should not be glossed over, for they represent the true cost of coal.

Note: In addition to the disasters discussed in this chapter, three explosions of firedamp occurred killing three miners about which there is very little information. These were as follows:

Richard Cousins	16	18 Mar 1828
Joseph Hodgson	41	30 Sept 1842
Charles Scandlin	?	17 Dec 1847

28th APRIL 1810

This is the first explosion in William Pit of which there is any recorded account, but when looking through the various documents and letters produced before and after the explosion, it was obvious that William was a very gassy pit and it was just a matter of time before it was to claim its first of many victims.

In his letter to Lord Lonsdale on the 26th February 1810, John Bateman, Lord Lonsdale's Agent, describes some of the work carried out in William Pit as follows:

> *"Last Saturday night, after all the workmen were gone out of Whingill Colliery, we forced the inflammable air out of the north part of William Pit*

(called Russia) now clear of water, and sent it up Harras Pit which is intended to be the upcast for William Pit".

Instead of removing the gas from the pit they were simply moving it about the workings. During the following month, the build-up of gas was so great in the "Low Eye" (the lowest working in the Shaft) that the workmen could not enter to carry out repair work; the Steel Mill would have been just as dangerous as the candle if its use had been sanctioned. The explosion was inevitable.....

It was in the Russia part of the pit on the Saturday, 28th, April, only two months later that the explosion took place. John Peile and Caleb Hetherington, who were the Colliery Viewers and four haggers were in the area which had been flooded for several months. Their task was to ensure the workings were properly ventilated by "turning the air" (making it take another course). Between three and four o'clock in the afternoon the gas fired and killed two of the workmen and burned the other four.

Two days after the explosion, John Bateman after clearing the gas from the workings had to convince the miners that the pit was now safe. He did this by sending his Overmen with some volunteer haggers, around the Russia area with lighted candles. He also stated that the dip workings (now full of inflammable air) was secured by all the doors in that part of the pit being nailed up to prevent any of the miners going into that part of the pit by mistake.

THE VICTIMS

Will Knowles	Hagger	Dead
John Gregg	Hagger	Dead
John Piele	Viewer	Burned
Caleb Hetherington	Viewer	Burned
William Green	Hagger	Burned
John Heslop	Hagger	Burned

13th APRIL 1821

This was the first explosion of any magnitude in William Pit, of which there is any detailed account. It occurred around noon on Friday 13th April 1821 and caused the death of five men employed as Haggers, and seven boys and girls employed as Drivers and Trappers. Five horses also perished, and three other youths were injured.

The workings had been inspected by an Overman only a quarter of an hour before the explosion occurred, and had been declared clear of gas. It was later ascertained that there had been a sudden and violent outburst of gas from the floor of the mine which was much broken up and fissured as a result of floor upheaval. This extraordinary outburst of Firedamp had undoubtedly come from a seam of coal, some six inches thick, located about eighteen feet below the Main Band. Several similar outbursts were to occur at later dates from the same seam, but with no loss of life. On examining the workings the following morning not a trace of gas could be found. The explosion was attributed to the ignition of the gas by a naked light, (a candle or candle lamp) although a Davy Safety Lamp was supplied to each hagger. Its use with the gauze correctly in place gave less light than that of a candle. If, when the outburst of Firedamp occurred, the gauze had been removed from a lamp, an explosion would take place before the gas could be detected. The cause of the explosion was blamed on the negligence of one of the men who died; it was surmised that he had mislaid his pick and in his haste to find it quickly, had removed the gauze from his lamp, so igniting the gas.

This then, was the first serious explosion in William Pit, and many more were to follow. It was also stated by interested members of the public that since the invention of the Davy Lamp, there had been a marked increase in explosions in the coal mines. This was attributed to the fact that miners could now fearlessly penetrate into workings which they dare not have explored with a candle; unfortunately the Davy Lamp gave such a poor light, that miners were sometimes tempted to remove the gauze...

The newspaper report at the time was very brief, and did not state what type of light had been issued to the Drivers and Trappers. It merely stated that every Hagger was provided with a safety lamp. The names of the dead were not given, only the number. There was no mention of any inquest. The names now given were taken from a document in the Whitehaven Records Office, and were further confirmed in the local Church Burial Registers.

THE VICTIMS

NAME	AGE	ADDRESS
John Coulthard	51	Newhouses
John Cragg	41	Newhouses
Margaret Froggat	?	?
John Gill	11	Parton
Dennis Hickey	31	Newhouses
Mary Hoy	16	Queen St
Christian Hoy	17	Queen St
George Hutchison	18	Newhouses
James McCave	26	Newhouses
Cecilia Morgan	19	Newhouses
James Scott	24	Kelsick Lane
Matthew Thornton	17	Newhouses

13th OCTOBER 1823

This explosion took place at six o'clock in the evening. The day shift workers were preparing to leave when a terrible explosion of Firedamp roared through the workings. It caused the instant death of fifteen men, fifteen boys, and two girls. The newspaper report on the disaster stated that seventeen horses 'of great value' also perished. Does this suggest that animals were valuable, and humans expendable?

According to the Stewards, the pit was well ventilated, and they assumed that the explosion probably resulted from negligence by one of the miners, who had ventured to remove the top of his Davy Lamp in a situation where the Firedamp was present. It was also suggested that some of the men had entered a prohibited area of the workings, but none of the bodies were actually found in such areas. Another possibility was that one of the miners had left his clothes in some corner of the workings, and on going to look for them, and for the sake of a better light, removed the top from his lamp and ignited the gas. These were only suggestions as to how the explosion took place, and if any inquest was held, the results were not published.

One interested member of the public wrote to the Whitehaven Gazette, and from his letter it would appear that he had made some inquiries himself. He mentioned that for weeks prior to the explosion, the miners were afraid to enter the workings, and many left to work in other pits rather than work where explosions were daily expected. Also that on the day of the explosion miners were working with lamps that were glowing red with the heat from the gas burning on the flame. It had been proven firedamp could be ignited by a red hot iron.

In many of the disasters in the Whitehaven pits there have been several instances when a son has died with his father, but this disaster must have been the one and only occasion when a daughter died with her dad: namely, Richard Bainbridge and his daughter Ann aged 11 years.

THE VICTIMS

NAME	AGE	ADDRESS
Richard Bainbridge	44	Soapery Court, Lady Pit
Ann Bainbridge	11	Ditto
John Blaylock	18	Newhouses
Matthew Blaylock	16	Ditto (Brothers)
John Cartmell	16	Bells Lane
John Corkan	16	Newhouses
William Cragg	15	Newhouses
Jonathan Dixon	41	Harras Moor
John Ellwood	17	Newhouses
Thomas Fitzpatrick	21	?
Fergus Frail	31	Newhouses
Mary Froggat	19	Newhouses
John Herring	14	Charles Street
James Hinde	43	Newhouses
Thomas Hughes	35	Ribton Lane
Thomas Irvin	41	Newhouses
John Leathers	17	Queen Street
Peter McAllister	52	Newhouses
William McCullock	16	Charles Street
John McGuire	45	Newhouses
Patrick McLaughlin	51	Newhouses (Father)
Archibald McLaughlin	16	Ditto (Son)
James McLellon	18	Newhouses
John McLellon	13	Ditto (Brothers)
Patrick Matthews	54	Newhouses
Patrick Marke	21	Newhouses
John Murray	?	Davy Pit
Christopher Pearson	17	Newhouses
William Sinclair	16	Quay Street
William Thompson	33	Aikbank
John Tweedie	16	?
Joseph Usher	?	Rosehill Gate

2nd JANUARY 1826 FIRE

This fire started in an area called "Old Engine District", where a 'Fire Engine' - a steam engine probably used for pumping operations, had been left working unattended for some time. Early that morning a group of seven miners discovered that some timber and coals near this engine had caught fire.

The air flowing through this area was vented via the upcast shaft of George Pit, which was situated in the triangle formed by Victoria Road, Coronation Drive and Brunlea Drive, near Sunny Hill. At the foot of the upcast shaft was the ventilating furnace, normally operated by two "firemen". However, fumes from the fire in Old Engine District had already suffocated these men. The furnace had burned its supply of fuel and gone out, thereby causing the air-flow in the workings to be reversed. The seven workmen who had discovered the fire presumably realised that there was a problem with the up-cast ventilation furnace and went to find out what had happened. Overcome by the fumes and lack of air, they also perished.

The rest of William Pit was not in any danger from this fire, as the district was isolated by dam doors situated in the connecting drift between George Pit upcast and the William Pit workings. These doors, which were of the same type as those installed in 1809 to prevent the inrush of water from North Pit (see chapter five) were firmly closed.

THE VICTIMS

Name	Age	Address
Thomas Flood	13	Newhouses
John Hanlin	69	?
Alexander Harris	40	Peter Street
John Lewthwaite	64	Newhouses
James Moor	78	Scotch Street
Edward Murray	18	George Pit
Daniel Paxton	30	Newhouses
Thomas Richardson	29	Newhouses
John Thompson	64	Newhouses

FEBRUARY 6th 1830

There was no official report of this explosion in the newspapers other than the inquest reported in the Cumberland Pacquet as follows:

WHITEHAVEN, Tuesday morning, February 9, 1830

"An inquest was held in this town on Saturday last, before P. Hodgson, Esq. coroner, on view of the bodies of three boys named Thomas Fox, Thomas Shields, and James Downie, who lost their lives by an explosion of firedamp in William Pit on the morning of that day. We understand that these youths were employed, two as drivers of horses with which they were leading water, and the other as a door opener, who it appears had neglected his duty and suffered a door of which he had the charge to remain open, thus cutting short the ventilation, and hence the unfortunate catastrophe which has been attended with such fatal consequences."

There is no mention of how the gas was ignited. Were the boys issued with Davy Lamps or were they using candles? If two of the boys were as stated "driving horses with which they were leading water", what happened to these horses? We know that the inquest was held to determine the cause of the deaths of the boys, but these were *valuable* horses as recorded in previous disasters. If they were using Davy Lamps, they could have only ignited the gas if one of them had removed the top from the lamp. If that was the case, then that should have been reported at the inquest. If they were using candles, what were they doing with naked lights in a part of the pit that could fill with gas so quickly if a door was left open? And finally, when an air door is left open the air to the workings inbye are deprived of air, but this is no danger to the trapper; *if he stays by his door*, he is still getting fresh air. So in order for the trapper to have been killed by the explosion, he must have moved inbye with the two drivers, leaving the door open....

None of these matters appear to have been considered at the Inquest. It is interesting to note that the Coroner who conducted the inquest, is the same person who in 1841 was reluctant to give information to Mr J.C.Symons, when he visited Whitehaven on behalf of "Her Majesties Commissioners" to report on the employment of women and children in the coal mines.

THE VICTIMS

NAME	AGE	ADDRESS
James Downie	14	Tangier Street
Thomas Fox	17	Newhouses
Thomas Shields	12	Newhouses

FEBRUARY 18th 1839

The explosion took place at 2 am, on Monday 18th February 1839, in the Main Band, about a mile and a half inbye in the direction of Parton.

The families and relatives of the William Pit miners flocked to the pit on hearing rumours that 50 men and boys and 40 horses had perished in a terrible explosion. Only three months previously the district had suffered a huge explosion at John Pit, located a half a mile outside the village of Lowca on the Harrington Road. Forty men and boys plus five horses had perished. With that disaster still fresh in the minds of the inhabitants of Whitehaven, it was all too easy for exaggerated rumours to gain ground.

On the Saturday night the Chief Overman examined that division of the mine in which the explosion took place, and found not the least trace of firedamp in any part of workings.

On Monday morning Joseph Topping, the Overman, had examined all the parts of the mine where the miners were to be employed but *not* the place where the explosion later occurred, and on completion of his examination set the miners to work. Topping then proceeded to that part of the mine which he had not yet examined. He was accompanied by a youth named Kennedy who was using an open oil lamp not a Davy Lamp. As they reached the area of the explosion, they entered the accumulation of firedamp, the gas fired and exploded in a direction away from Topping and Kennedy thus allowing them to escape with their lives, although badly burned. The explosion was to claim the lives of twenty three men and boys and two horses. By 6 o'clock that evening all the bodies had been brought to the surface. It was a mournful and heart rending spectacle to witness the removal of the bodies, as they were taken through the streets in the horse and carts, to their respective homes, followed by sorrowing relatives and crowds of people.

The inquest was held the following day and was conducted by the coroner Mr. Peter Hodgson. After a Jury had been appointed and sworn in their first task was to visit the homes of the deceased to view the bodies. The first house visited was the home of the Tear brothers, James (18) and Robert (12). The features of the corpses were calm and undisturbed, indicating that death had been instantaneous, and that they had passed away without a struggle.

Most of the other corpses presented an appearance similar to that of the two Tears. Some of the bodies were so little altered that it was difficult to realise that they were the victims of such a dreadful fate. The faces and breasts of others, however, were scorched and burned. Some of them had apparently suffered terribly, and their aspect was awful in the extreme. This was particularly the case with George Scott aged 60, and a boy aged 13, named Michael Wheatley, both of whom were lying in one bed. These two had evidently been exposed to the full fury of the blast face on; every aspect of humanity was obliterated, and replaced by the most awful and horrid appearance of which the human mind can form any conception.

In order to discover the cause of the explosion, and the cause of the deaths of the victims, several witnesses were called. These are the statements of the two most important witnesses.

William Thornton, Overman:

> *The Tears were brothers, and lived in Nicholson Alley. I did not see all the bodies as they came up, but I saw the Tears, and they were a little burned. The men were mostly killed by suffocation, but some of them were slightly burned. I am an overman at William Pit, and my duty is to see that the ventilation is kept good, and that everything is in proper order. I examined the pit the last time on Saturday morning. I went through it all, and found it quite right. I found the ventilation was good at that time, and that it was in a capital state of safety. I first heard of the explosion about a quarter past three o'clock on Monday morning. I immediately dressed myself, and went down into the pit. I saw nothing particular at the bottom of the shaft, and I proceeded to examine the workings. I proceeded about a mile, and found everything correct at that distance. The air was good at the distance of a mile; but I here found that some doors were blown away, which we got up as soon as possible for the purpose of carrying the air forward. I then proceeded about a mile further and found four or five doors blown away. I got temporary doors fixed, and by this means we got a supply of good air. I proceeded five or six hundred yards further, and found several stoppings blown out, which we replaced with wood. We then went on to two doors which were standing good, we opened them and proceeded about sixty yards further, and found another stopping blown out. Here we found the corpse of a boy named Levi Hoskin, lying on the pavement on his face. The boy was not burned that I could discover. I proceeded on still and found the bodies of three other boys. Richardson Shields, William Atkinson, and, I believe John Ross. I went on further and found a horse lying dead. I proceeded and found three other boys lying, Christopher Pearson, William Doran, and John Donald, who were all suffocated. In going forward I found a horse dying. I went on still further, and found a man alive, John Develyn, who was lying on the pavement, with his safety lamp burning by his side. Felix M'Ginnis was lying dead beside him. I went further on, and found Richard Harrison, John Tordiff, John Firth, and a boy I did not know. I proceeded a little further and found Hugh Roney, William Smith,*

Barney Cairn, and William Davidson, all dead. I saw no more corpses in the pit. I went further, where I saw two others nearly suffocated, They were Joseph Topping, and Thomas Kennedy. We got them all to the bottom of the shaft, and had them drawn up, and for anything I know to the contrary, they are all living yet. The circumstance of the doors being blown away was indicative of a blast. I had much difficulty in breathing, and the air was bad, when I was at the furthermost point from the shaft. One of the Tears seemed slightly burned, but not sufficient, as I thought to cause death."

The coroner and jury then proceeded to Joseph Topping's house, near William Pit, they found him in a weak and dangerous state, but perfectly sensible, and willing to be examined:

" I am a miner, and was in William Pit on the morning of the accident, a boy named Kennedy went with me, and we went about two miles from the bottom of the pit, where the accident happened. The boy had a patent lamp and a common lantern in his hand, there was an oil light in the lantern which was open. I considered this place perfectly safe. Between half past two and three o'clock the inflammable air became ignited. If I had suspected any danger I would not have gone in. After an explosion of firedamp, unless a person working at the place makes his escape, he cannot live. Immediately after an explosion or blast, air is produced in which we cannot live. I am satisfied that from the effects of the ignition of the inflammable air, and the blasts consequent thereupon, the individuals who lost their lives in William Pit, yesterday, were killed by the ignition of inflammable air, or by the choke damp consequent upon the explosion, by which they were suffocated, and the whole catastrophe was accidental and not occasioned by any negligence or want of skill whatever."

Topping's statement attempts to suggest that the explosion was purely accidental. Yet he had walked into a working full of firedamp without testing to see if it was clear. Firedamp is lighter than normal air, and when released from the coal, it accumulates in the roof. If the gas was ignited by the lantern, held at waist level, the workings must have been full of gas and not just in the roof.

The workings had last been examined on Saturday night. On Monday morning at 2am, Topping as the Overman in charge of the workings, should never have allowed anyone carrying a naked flame into the workings before he had examined them to ensure that no gas was present.

It was later found that build-up of the firedamp was the result of an outburst of gas from small coal seam below the Main Band seam, the floor of the workings lifting and allowing the gas to escape. The verdict of the Jury was accidental death in all cases with the following recommendation:

> *"That in future, no person be allowed to use a lamp, the flame whereof shall be exposed so as to come into contact with the air, and advise that in future, greater caution shall be observed in that respect."*

Because of the state of some of the bodies they were buried as soon as the jury had viewed them, and the remainder on the following day, including that of Felix McGinnis who had given his life in rescuing John Develyn. They were all accompanied to their graves by members of the Miners' Society, each of whom wore a white hat band on the occasion. The expenses of the funerals were born by the Earl of Lonsdale, who also gave instructions to provide the widows and families of all the deceased colliers with a free cottage and free coals, and an allowance of two shillings (10p) per week.

THE VICTIMS

Name	Age	Address
William Atkinson	14	Newtown
Barney Cairn	24	Tangier Street
Joseph Clark	14	Newhouses
William Davidson	41	Newhouses
William Doran	14	Newhouses
John Dunn	11	Newhouses
John Firth	33	Charles Street
John Fisher	10	Newhouses
Thomas Gilmore	60	Tangier Street
Richard Harrison	43	Newhouses
Levi Hoskins	16	Rosemary Lane
Felix M'Ginnis	33	Tangier Street
William McMullen	11	Newhouses
Christopher Pearson	14	Newhouses
Hugh Raney	46	Banks Lane
John Ross	16	Charles Street
George Scott	60	Newhouses
Richardson Shields	16	Newhouses
William Smith	22	Newhouses
James Tear	18	Addisons Alley
Robert Tear	12	Ditto (Brothers)
John Tordiff	31	Newhouses
Michael Wheatley	13	Newhouses

12th MARCH 1850

It would appear from the evidence given at the inquest conducted by the coroner Mr. William Lumb, Esq., and from documents held at the Whitehaven Records office, that this explosion of Firedamp was avoidable.

Two colliers, William Pearson and Bernard Carr were working in a part of William Pit which was so well ventilated that that they were working with the tops of their Davy lamps off. This practice was allowed if the Waster or Viewer found the working free of gas and gave permission to do so. From the evidence given, Pearson and Carr decided to look at some old pillars of coal which were in an abandoned, unventilated part of the district. To get to these old workings, they had to put themselves to great trouble and inconvenience and virtually crawl some seventy or eighty yards along the very low roadway. They had been told not to enter the workings, primarily because the area was not ventilated. Not only did they ignore the warning, but entered the workings with the tops of their Davy lamps removed.

Another collier, Daniel Graham, said he was working near to where the two had entered and felt the blast of the explosion. He immediately replaced the top of his lamp and ran towards the sound of the blast. On the way he met the Under Steward, William Golightly. They shouted then heard the two men answer. Both were badly burned and were got out of the pit immediately. They were taken to Miners' Infirmary on the Back Row, Newhouses. Nurse Catherine McKenzie confirmed that they were brought to the Infirmary on Tuesday 12th March. William Pearson died on Friday and Bernard Carr a few days later.

In a letter to Lord Lonsdale giving details of the accident, Mr Bourne the Colliery Viewer, was of the opinion that if the two men had worn flannel shirts as was the directive of the management, they would have suffered less burns and most probably survived.

THE VICTIMS

Name	Age	Address
William Pearson	26	Newtown
Bernard Carr	?	?

25th APRIL 1882

On the night of the 25th April, 1882, five men were at work in the Countess District. Three of them were at work near to the bottom of a stone drift, pumping out the water from the inbye workings. The other two were haggers about to start work at the face in a heading further inbye from the pump. Only one of these five, Edward Martin was to survive the explosion that took place that night.

The Countess District was exploiting completely new measures, and a considerable quantity of gas was being encountered. Colliers in this area were issued with "Geordie" lamps which were considered even safer than the normal Davy Lamp.

The air that was ventilating the Countess District had already travelled more than two and a half miles before reaching these workings, and was conducted to the headings by bratticing.

At seven o'clock Thomas Williamson, the Deputy-Overman, examined the workings which he declared safe and set the men to work. Three men - Henry Finch, John McGuinness and Thomas Colvin, were operating the pump, and the two haggers were James Geddes and Edward Martin.

The two haggers prepared to start work. They placed their lamps, one on top of a 'copy' (stool) and the other one on the base of an upturned bucket. They started to take their top clothing off when Martin saw that the gas had been ignited and was burning in the roof. Seeing their danger, Martin and Geddes seized their lamps and ran out. They ran a distance of about thirty yards before they were struck down by the force of the explosion. Martin, though considerably injured, succeeded getting out to the top of the stone drift, beyond which point the ventilation system had not been destroyed by the explosion. Geddes was unable to get any further than the point where he was eventually found and died shortly afterwards. Martin managed to get to the pit top then walked home.

One of the rescuers described their efforts as follows:

> *"I hurried with all speed to the pit top. I descended with others to endeavour to restore the ventilation. On arriving at what is called the Countess District, better known as the Crosscuts, we found that it was at this place that the explosion took place, and found Messrs. G.H.Liddel, R.W.Moore, W. Harker, Southern, James and John Rothery, A Henderson, A. Wilkinson, J.E.Elwood, J Wilkinson, R.Harker, H. Johnstone, W. Muncaster, and others actively superintending the*

movements of the joiners, in getting the brattice carried into the drift. On getting it in a distance of say 80 yards we came upon the body of Thomas Colvin, at 10.45 a.m., partly sitting, and lying on his right side. I examined his features, and found he looked as placid as if he were asleep, all signs of life being extinct. I may mention he had his coat thrown over his head to partly save him from the fire. On going over a distance of perhaps a dozen yards or more, we found the body of Henry Finch, lying on his face, the arms and body being frightfully burned. We next found the body of John McGuinness, which was badly burned too, but neither of them sufficiently to cause death, which must have been caused by the after-damp. We then brought the bodies to the bank, (pit top) *arriving there about 12.55, the bodies being placed in the overman s office to await the coroner's inquest."*

The inquest was opened by Mr. W. Lumb, the Coroner for the district, and adjourned until the 2nd June 1882, when the circumstances under which the explosion happened, and the state of the mine at the time of the fatal accident occurred were considered. The Jury's verdict was that:

1. That the deaths were accidental.
2. That no one was to blame.

The cause was possibly that one of the hagger's lamps was faulty.

Arnold Morley, MP, who attended the inquest on behalf of the Secretary of State, was not satisfied that no-one was to blame. After listening to the evidence, and reading deputies and overmen's reports covering the weeks prior to the explosion, he was concerned about the ventilation of the Countess District, and summed up his report as follows:

"The system which was in use in the Countess District, of depending upon brattice for the ventilation of so great a length of underground working, especially at such a distance from the shaft, must be described as unsatisfactory and unsafe, and although, while the stone drift was being made, and until another communication could be opened up, it might have been necessary, no time should have elapsed before such a communication was effected, and it is certainly open to question whether any men should have been allowed in any part of the workings except those actually employed in carrying it out.

In the present case two months had passed without anything being done, and the two men, Martin and Geddes, were working at the coal as ordinary haggers, and not in connection with the proposed alteration in the system of ventilation.

But in addition to this, these men were allowed to work in that part of the mine when it was known that considerable quantities of gas were in the immediate neighbourhood, and when, apart from the unsatisfactory system of ventilation, the existence of such a danger should have pointed to great caution.

In conclusion, I have to submit, for consideration to the Secretary of State, whether proceedings should not be taken against the certified manager, Mr. William Harker, under section 32 of the Coal Mines Regulations Act, 1872; or whether a prosecution should not be instituted against him and one or more of the officials of the mine under the said act for the breach of G.R., No. 1, of section 51.

14th July 1882

Arnold Morley"

As a result of this report and at a special court of the Whitehaven Magistrates on Tuesday 15th August 1882, Mr. Gerrard Henry Liddell, Agent of the Whitehaven Colliery, and Mr. William Harker, Manager of William Pit, were charged with "Neglect of duty in respect of the rules laid down for their guidance in the Coal Mines Regulation Act."

The hearing lasted the one day, the bench retired for a few minutes on their return the Chairman said: "The Bench are of opinion that there is no evidence in either case upon which a conviction could follow, and we therefore dismiss them both."

THE VICTIMS

Killed

Name	Age	Address
Thomas Colvin	67	Parton
Henry Finch	33	High Windsor, Harras Moor.
James Geddes	30	35, Castle Row, Newhouses.
John McGuinness	21	55, Back Row, Newhouses.

Injured

John Graham	?	Middle Row, Newhouses.
James Halliwell	50	Coach Road.
Edward Martin	30	20, Front Row, Newhouses.
David Slatery	21	M'Garry's Buildings.
William Taggart	21	Mount Pleasant.

26th NOVEMBER 1907

This was the first of the William Pit explosions to be caused by the use of explosives for shot-firing.

The explosion occurred at 1.50 p.m. at the face of a stone drift, which had been driven for a quarter of a mile off the intake airway and endless rope haulage road leading to the Lowca and Countess districts in the Main Band seam.

Several men were working about four hundred yards from the face of the drift when the explosion occurred. They were William Cannon, William Cowan, Evan Evans, John Hanlon, Joseph Kennedy, and Thomas Moore. They were engaged in putting some full tubs on the road when the force of the explosion hurled them off their feet, killing Kennedy and injuring the others. W Cowan stated:

> *"I was standing sideways when the explosion occurred. The concussion and flames were terrible. I was thrown down and for a short time was unconscious, but recovered to feel a burning and choking sensation. We were all similarly affected."*

At the end of the drift and on the main intake a number of hewers were waiting for the riding set. They felt the force of the blast but no-one was injured. As soon as word reached the pit top, the Colliery Manager with several officials went underground to organise the rescue operations. There was no shortage of volunteers from the miners already in the pit including the hewers who felt the blast of the explosion. By 3.30 p.m. despite the drift and part of the intake being contaminated with dense fumes and choking coal dust, the injured had been put into tubs or on stretchers and brought outbye to the pit top. Dr George Harris arrived at the pit top soon after the first of the injured emerged. He later went down the pit in order to render whatever aid he could.

Most of the injured were treated and removed to their homes. John Hanlon, and Thomas Moore were taken to the Infirmary; Hanlon had a broken right leg, broken ribs, and head injuries whilst Moore's injuries included a very bad scalp wound.

Meanwhile the rescuers underground were still struggling in the dense fumes to find the other miners known to be near or in the drift. By 6.00 p.m. the bodies of William Fitzsimmons and Joseph Kennedy were brought to the surface and taken to their homes.

This still left three miners unaccounted for. They were Alfred Burns, William Hanlon, and James Rowe, and it was known that they had been near the face of the drift when the explosion occurred. As a result of the violence of the explosion the rescuers encountered three falls of roof as they fought their way into the drift. One was thirty yards in length, the next ten, and a third about eight yards. All these had to be re-timbered to allow safe passage to and from the workings beyond.

The rescuers finally reached the bodies of the three miners at about 7.20 p.m. on Wednesday evening. They lay together behind an empty tub. Burns, who was the shot firer, lay between the tub and the right side of the road, his face against the floor, covered by his hands. Hanlon and Rowe were lying across the road against the inner end of the tub. They were all severely burned, their hair was nearly all singed off, and strips of skin were hanging loose.

By half past nine the bodies had been brought up the shaft and conveyed to their respective homes on stretchers by their fellow workmen, followed by a number of friends and sympathisers.

At the inquest held on January 7th 1908, the jury gave it's verdict as follows:

> *"The jury are of the opinion that the five men lost their lives in No 6 Drift, William Pit, by an explosion of gas, but how it occurred, there is not sufficient evidence to show. But they are also of opinion that there was not sufficient ventilation."*

In his report on the explosion, Mr. J. B. Atkinson, Chief Inspector of Mines, came to the following conclusions:

> *"Although the jury did not so find, it was not disputed that the flame causing the explosion arose from the firing of a blown out shot in the coal seam, and as already indicated there may be some suspicion as to the nature of the stemming used to stem the shot-hole or whether it was stemmed at all. The cause of the explosion was undoubtedly firedamp which must have been present in considerable quantity, and it is difficult to conceive how it had escaped the notice of the persons in the drift.*
>
> *As already stated, the flame from the explosion did not reach the engine plane which contained coal dust (due to the carriage of coal against the air current). This dust was raised in dense clouds by the explosion, and as already stated caused much inconvenience to the persons exposed to it, and had the flame reached the haulage road the loss of life would have been very great, as probably the whole morning shift amounting to 180 persons inbye of the "friction gear," would have lost their lives."*

THE VICTIMS

Killed

Name	Age	Address
Alfred Burns	36	Countess Terrace, Bransty
William V Fitzsimmons	22	Hugh Street, Bransty
William Hanlon	30	Charles Street, Whitehaven
James Rowe	24	George Street, Whitehaven
Joseph Kennedy	22	Brydens Court Queen, Whitehaven

Injured

Evan Evans	?	Scotch Street, Whitehaven
William Cowan	?	Countess Terrace, Bransty
John Nelson	?	Parton
William Cannon	?	Irish Street, Whitehaven
Thomas Moore	?	Mark Lane, Whitehaven
John Hanlon	?	Queen Street, Whitehaven

Note: John and William Hanlon were brothers.

It may be of interest to the reader to know that the most disastrous explosion on record was also caused by a blown-out shot in a heading, which raised and ignited a cloud of coal dust. This was at Courrieres in France in 1906, when 1,100 men and 98 horses were killed.

11th JULY 1922

This was the second explosion in William Pit that involved the firing of shots.

The explosion occurred on a Tuesday night when two workers were involved in shot-firing in a new drift in the Delaval District, three and a half miles from the shaft bottom. The victims, John Rogan who was the Shot-Firer, and Patrick Kilbane a Charge-Hand, remained behind at the conclusion of the shift for the purpose of firing shots, and were the only workers in a new drift in that district when the accident occurred.

Albert Atherton, Drifter, who lived at 8 Low Road, Whitehaven, had been working in the drift filling metal. About 10 o'clock he left to go outbye, leaving Rogan and Kilbane in the drift preparing to fire the shots. He stopped near to an air compressor when he heard the first shot fired. Five minutes later he was still at the compressor when he was bowled over by the force of an explosion. He made his way outbye for about 150 yards when he met the manager Mr. Brodie coming inbye with some men. He went with them back towards the drift. The badly-scorched bodies of Rogan and Kilbane were found. Death appeared to have been instantaneous. A crowd had gathered at the pit yard upon hearing of the accident, and the bodies were brought to the surface in the early hours of Wednesday morning.

At the inquest held at the Whitehaven Police Court on the 19th July 1922, Mr. Wilson, HM Chief Inspector of Mines, said that he had no doubt in his mind that the explosion had been caused by firedamp being ignited by a blown-out shot. The gas that had been ignited had accumulated because the brattice had been damaged during the firing of previous shots and had not been detected.

The jury returned a verdict that the deceased were killed in an accidental explosion of gas, and were of the opinion that 'sufficient and careful examination' of the drift was not always made.

THE VICTIMS

Name	**Age**	**Address**
Patrick Kilbane	30	Queen Street
John Rogan	47	15 Gores Buildings

3rd JUNE 1941

This explosion was unique in the history of the William Pit explosions, and perhaps in the history of coal mining. It was not caused by firedamp or coal dust, but by a combination of spontaneous combustion and water gas. There had in fact been two instances of explosions caused in this way at pits elsewhere, but in neither case had lives been lost.

When coal in a seam which is liable to spontaneous combustion (Gob Fire) starts to oxidise, the coal pillars which have not been extracted undergo a chemical re-action and start to increase in temperature. Unless this is brought under control, the temperature continues to rise, producing a progressive increase in the oxidation rate. When the temperature reaches about 7O C (158 F), a crucial change takes place in the oxidation rate which leads to spontaneous combustion.

At this stage if sufficient ventilation can be provided, heat generated by oxidation can be dissipated, reducing the temperature and preventing any *further* rise in the rate of oxidation. Alternatively, if ventilation is positively witheld, and the area deprived of new air, the existing oxygen will quickly be consumed and further oxidation prevented. Unless one or other of these two very different strategies is implemented quickly then spontaneous combustion will ensue.

Modern methods of mining ensure that seams that are liable to spontaneous combustion have a simple layout, capable of being quickly isolated and effectively sealed off. But this was not the case with William Pit. By 1941 the pit had been mining coal for 130 years. Thousands of yards of old roadways, passages, and pillars of coal left in to support the roof in the Main and Bannock Bands had been sealed off, but for many years it had been recognised that Main Band was liable to spontaneous combustion.

Water Gas had never before been heard of in William Pit. "Water Gas" is produced when water is poured or sprayed over burning coals. Water contains Oxygen and Hydrogen, and when heated to a point where steam is given off, the gases separate. Oxygen is not itself combustible - it only *supports* combustion, whereas Hydrogen is a highly combustible gas with an explosive range of between 3% to 70% concentration; once it is formed and a source of ignition is available, it will explode.

Heatings or fires had occurred on several occasions prior to 1941. Outbreaks had been sealed off in the Main Band in 1911, 1918 and 1924, and in 1928 the workings in the Main Band inbye Lowca Junction were abandoned and sealed off. These seals it was noted, were getting further outbye towards the Lowca Junction each time they were built. In other words the fires and heatings were forcing the men outbye in a kind of retreating action.

By December 1938 it was realised that they were fighting a losing battle with the heatings. It was then decided to appoint Mr. A. B. Dawson who held a First Class Managers Certificate to take charge of all operations in connection with gob fires. He had under him two practically full-time deputies on the day shift and one on the afternoon shift, together with considerable staff of workmen who rarely numbered less than 20, and at times more than 100. To employ that number of staff and workers on the gob fires, proves just how critical the situation had become.

By the end of March 1940 further signs of active combustion was found at one of the stoppings when smoke was seen issuing from breaks in its left side. Steps were at once taken to strengthen it to prevent leakages of the smoke into airways. This entailed cutting into the sides of the roadway to find unfractured coal. Dense smoke issued from the breaks, smouldering coal was encountered and very high temperatures were registered. It was clear that very active combustion in the immediate neighbourhood of this stopping was taking place.

Three months later on 22nd July 1940 a fire was detected to the *front* of a stopping. This external fire was extinguished and the hot material cooled down by the use of water, but a small hole a few inches square was revealed between the brickwork and the coal side, and through it the coal along the hole and inside the stopping could be seen glowing bright red.

On the morning of 3rd June 1941, the gob fire team of workmen resumed work on a new stopping in an area of the Main Band directly underneath the Countess Bannock Front Drift. Water was applied to some rubble on the outbye side of the existing old stopping that was warm but not hot. After soaking the rubble, the water ran out into an old roadway and drained away so completely that no further trace of it could be found. It was obvious that it must have found some way through the floor of the roadway and into the old workings. By then the water had been running for at least 45 minutes at an estimated rate of 30 gallons per minute and had not re-appeared at the point where they expected to find it.

The Manager, Mr. Farquhar and Mr. Dawson, who were visiting the site of the new stopping along with The Deputy Mr. G. Savage, withdrew to go outbye. The workmen had already gone, their shift being ended. The time was then between 1.15 and 1.30 p.m.. The water was left running, the door in the new stopping was left open, and the doors in the air-lock were closed.

At about 2.15 p.m. the back shift in the Countess Bannock District was pursuing its normal course. The Countess Bannock main haulage road leading to the coal faces was almost directly above the area of the stopping and airlock.

Shortly after this time a violent explosion occurred among the old pillars of the Main Band seam. Such was the violence of the explosion that it blew a hole upwards through five feet of strata and into the main haulage road of the Countess Bannock Band. The explosion left a hole five feet in diameter and continued outbye killing and injuring miners near the Lowca Junction, and inbye killing and injuring miners near the entrance to the No 2 Dip Face. As a result of the explosion twelve miners died and eleven were injured.

The Manager, Mr. Farquhar, Mr. Dawson and the Deputy, G. Savage, were proceeding outbye on foot. They were just over half way out to the shaft bottom when the explosion occurred. They merely felt a temporary reversal of the air current which caused them to immediately return inbye. It took them 30 minutes to reach Lowca Junction and immediately encountered indications of violence, signal wires were down, and props supporting the roof had been blown out and were lying about. The haulage rope was still running, because the engine driver had been injured, and was in no condition to halt it. Whilst the Manager went to cut off the power to the haulage engine, Mr. Dawson went towards the stopping area. At the airlock he found that the doors had been blown away and smoke was issuing from the brick work and he could go no further. The separation doors in the Lowca Level were burning fiercely. There was a mass of wrecked tubs at the bottom of Countess Bannock Drift.

Arrangements for the recovery and evacuation of the injured were speedily put into operation, and by 4.00p.m. they were either out of the pit or well on the way in that direction. By 9.00p.m.the last of the bodies had been taken to the surface and the area cleared.

During the rescue operations in the Countess Bannock Drift it was noted that at a point about 30 yards up the drift there was a hole about 5 feet in diameter in the floor on the left hand side. The tram rails over the hole had been blown vertically upwards and an extensive fire was raging below and dense smoke was issuing from the hole. By 9.00 p.m., when all the men in the workings at the time of the explosion had been accounted for and all the dead bodies evacuated, the fire inside the airlock in the Main Band had reached such dimensions that any hopes of fighting it was out of the question. By 10.00p.m., all the officials and workmen had left the mine.

At about 2.30 a.m. on Wednesday 4th June, the Managing Director of the Company arrived from Glasgow together with two mining advisors. Shortly afterwards a small party, including the General Manager, Mr. J. Williamson, one of the mining experts and three of HM Inspectors descended the pit and proceeded to Lowca Junction. Previous opinions on the futility of attempting to combat the fire were confirmed. It was then decided to seal off the district. This operation was successfully completed by the building of dams in the intake and return airways 1,400 yards outbye from the fire area. In sealing off the whole district, any evidence that would have been useful at the inquiry into the explosion was lost for ever.

The inquiry opened at Whitehaven on Tuesday 29th July 1941. Mr. F. H. Wynne, HM Chief Inspector of Mines, presided. Men and youths, some still heavily bandaged as a result of their injuries, were among those who gave evidence.

A witness who was congratulated by the President and others in the manner in which he gave evidence was Thomas J. Fox, an 18 year old haulage hand, who had worked in William Pit for three years. He told how he had been working with John Burney who subsequently lost his life. Burney and he took turns at alternate ends of the line of tubs, and he was going to the end of a set when something seemed to pick him up and throw him back. It was like a blast of wind. He was facing the blast and was knocked flat on his back. Burney crawled over to him and said "Come on I think something's gone west." Hanging on to one another, he and Burney started making their way to Lowca Junction. They could not make it because the dust was starting to choke them. They turned back and had to get into a manhole to allow a full run-away set to go past them. They got out of the manhole and Fox lost Burney. He thought he saw Moses Stephens lying at the side. He then tried to get out via Countess Drift but it was too hot to breathe, so he had to go back a second time. He lost consciousness and on coming round he was sick twice and then, as the air cleared, he felt better and got out.

(Note: this same Thomas J. Fox was to die six years later in the William Pit explosion of 1947).

Henry Shepherd, Rope Splicer, was working in Lowca Level repairing a haulage rope. He heard a strange bump, something that he had never heard before, so he made his way to Lowca Junction which was thick with dust. He had to pass through two sets of doors to get to the Junction but found that they would not open. He forced the doors with a bar and when he got through the atmosphere was so thick that he passed the Junction and was into Delaval Level without knowing it. Stumbling along he fell over something and found it was a man. He shook him and spoke to him but got no reply. He found the bodies of three other men but could not recognise them. As he went along the main road to telephone for help he met the rescue workers headed by Mr. Farquhar.

Benjamin Cowan, 29, a Deputy, said when he went into the district he found that three of his workers were not at the place where they should have been working. He asked other men where the three were. They said there had been "a puff of wind" and the three had gone to investigate. Cowan then went to look for the men and along the road he encountered fumes. He came across the Overman, Isaac Graham, who had been knocked out. With McClusky and Skelly, Cowan forced his way through some doors and took Graham to the top of No 2 Dip. He saw Moses Stephens and James George lying with the haulage rope pinning them down, but the rope was too tight to lift. He also saw Wells and Harker lying together, but was not sure whether they were also trapped by the rope. At Lowca Junction the air was clear but the doors were burning. At Delaval there was some smouldering and a flame burst out. This was put out with a fire extinguisher.

In his report on the causes of death of the victims, Dr. V. C. H. Harris gave the following details:

Carbon monoxide poisoning and injuries	3
Carbon monoxide poisoning and blast	1
Blast and burns	6
Blast, burns and injuries	1
Severe injuries	1

With a history of explosions which few coal mines could match, it was only natural that this latest explosion in the William Pit should be assumed to be yet another caused by firedamp. In this instance, however, it was a false assumption. Throughout a period of two and a half years from the first detection of carbon monoxide in the return airway near the "Humbug Doors" to the day of the explosion, Firedamp had never been met with any sufficient quantity to be detected on the flame of a safety lamp (less than one and a quarter percent) in the vicinity of any of the operations involved during the building of the stoppings or subsequently, either on the intake or return side.

In his summing up of the enquiry Mr, F. H. Wynne made the following statement:

> *"Such an explosion cannot occur unless there are concurrent (a) a large mass of red hot carbonaceous or coaly material; (b) a supply of water which on conversion to steam remains for an appreciable time in close contact with hot carbon, (c) partial confinement to a space in which mixture of the water-gas takes place and (d) contact with the explosive mixture of water-gas and air with some igniting medium. These essentials are not likely to occur except when a fire is deep seated in a mass of coal.*
>
> *While it may perhaps be dangerous to dogmatise, the opinion is here definitely expressed that in the case of deep-seated spontaneous fires, treatment by water can only be promiscuous and it may also be hazardous.*

In any event, water cannot be relied upon as a curative unless it is applied in such quantity as to cause complete immersion. The William Pit explosion is a striking example of this thesis."

THE VICTIMS

Killed

Name	Age	Address
Sydney Barbour	21	25 Queen Street Whitehaven
Robert Baxter	55	5 Coniston Road Woodhouse
John P. Burney	20	Bentick Row Ginns
Jonathan Curwen	57	North Row Kells
James George	18	49 Fell View Avenue Woodhouse
William Harker	20	Countess Terrace Bransty
Charles Martin	45	South View Road Bransty
Robert McGrievy	19	50 Valley View Road Greenbank
Cornelius Moore	40	34 Scotch Street Whitehaven
James O'Pray	37	80 Bransty Road Bransty
William Perry	50	28 South View Road Bransty
James Wells	28	9 Charles Street Whitehaven

Injured

John R. Baxter Jnr	29	17 Tangier Street Whitehaven
William Benson	29	Reids Court Scotch Street Whitehaven
John Fitzsimmons	21	17 Back Ginns Whitehaven
Richard D. Glaister	45	13 Lakeland Avenue Seacliffe
Isaac Graham	51	The Green Bransty
W. J. Kerr	44	1 Mill Street Whitehaven
George Porterhouse	50	16 North Road Bransty
Joseph Rogan*	18	99 Queen Street Whitehaven
Henry Ruddick	60	6 Countess Terrace, Bransty
Moses Stephens	17	50 Fell View Avenue Woodhouse

***(Note:** Joseph Rogan was subsequently killed by a roof fall in Haig Pit, 27th February 1959).

15th AUGUST 1947

This was the third of the explosions to be caused by shot-firing. It would be the last explosion in William Pit's 150 year history, and the second worst disaster in the history of coal mining in Cumberland.

As a result of the 1941 explosion and the danger of further spontaneous combustion, the Main and Bannock Band seams had been sealed off, leaving only the Six Quarters Seam in production. Since the re-opening of the Whitehaven Collieries in 1937 the coal at William Pit had been worked by the "Longwall" method of mining. These were advancing machine-cut, hand-filled conveyor longwall faces. (See glossary of mining terms) The face was worked over a 24 hour cycle using three shifts. Coal filling, haulage and coal winding were done on the day shift. Pan-pulling, brushing and packing, and coal cutting on the back shift. Back brushing and general repairs on the night shift.

The explosion was caused by the firing of a "Cuckoo Shot" on No. 2 Dip Right Side Face. On a longwall face when all the coal is extracted as the face advances, the space left behind is called the "Goaf". In order to support the roof of the goaf, stone 'packs' filled with rubble were built. These were 4 yards in width and 8 yards apart, and are extended each day as the face advanced. The packs were built with the stone from the unsupported roof that falls between the the packs. It was a generally accepted practice that had been used for the past six months, to induce the roof to fall by firing shot-holes that had been bored into the roof towards the goaf; these were known as "Cuckoo Shots".

On Friday, 15th August, 1947, 118 men had started their work on the back shift. On No. 2 Dip Right Side Face in the Six Quarters Seam the brushers, coal cutters, packers and pan pullers were at work and the Shot Firer was firing some Cuckoo Shots. At 5.40 p.m. whilst firing one of these shots, the pit exploded.

The first warning that something had happened was when the onsetter at the pit bottom felt "a rush of wind" coming from inbye which raised the dust. Although the blast was quite strong, it did not knock him over, but he knew at once that something serious had happened, and immediately 'phoned the pit top.

The Manager, Mr W. H. McAllister, had left the pit a few minutes before the onsetter had made his warning call, and on reaching home received an urgent message to return to the pit at once. All he was told was that something had happened, so he immediately descended the pit. He was not long in coming to the conclusion that there had been an explosion and put the emergency procedures into action, to which all responded without delay.

The Manager then went inbye along the main intake road to explore. Meeting some workmen, he took them with him. (See Stephen Ferguson's story) He had not gone very far when he noticed a peculiar smell which, from previous experience, he associated immediately with an explosion. On reaching the 'air crossing' from the Six Quarters Seam to the main return in the Main Band Seam, he sent two workmen to examine the doors and the state of the air in the return, with a view to reaching two repairers, Fox and Marshall, who had been sent to work in the main return by the deputy, Stephen Ferguson. They reported that the doors were intact, and that the air was deadly, so any attempt at rescue without breathing apparatus was impossible. Two workmen, Billy Adair and Johnny McGordon, were at once sent to the shaft to bring in canaries and a portable reviving apparatus. The remainder of the party proceeded inbye.

R.A.F. Police dog Joins the Search

Rex, seen here with his master, Flight Lieutenant R.D. Cooper, (left) and a mines rescue worker, was one of three dogs belonging to the R.A.F. used to find the bodies of victims of the 1947 disaster.

The air doors in the the connecting roadway between intake and return in the Six Quarters Seam were intact, but from this point inbye, signs that a violent explosion had taken place became more evident, and the smell in the atmosphere more noticeable. The party pressed on. When the junction with Old No. 2 North was reached, they found tubs derailed, roof girders displaced and the roof weighting badly.

After setting some workmen on to strengthen the roof supports, the party moved on again but found the roadway dangerous because of numerous falls. The party then returned to the junction of Old No. 2 North District and found intake air entering it. This roadway had been previously sealed off by a brick stopping with two half doors in it. At the air crossing itself, there were two doors leading into the main return. One was blown off and the other blown open and damaged. The return airway was heavily fouled with deadly afterdamp. About this time the first of the rescue teams arrived.

The canaries were tried in the return airway and immediately collapsed and died in their cages. Because of falls and dangerous roof conditions, access to the 107 trapped miners was impossible, and since the only possible approach to the inbye workings was by way of the return airway, which was fouled by the poisonous afterdamp, all exploration and recovery work was carried out by fully equipped rescue teams.

All the reports from the rescue teams covering the night of the explosion and the following morning, which gave details as to the conditions prevailing in the inbye workings of the Six Quarters Seam gave no grounds for hope that the trapped miners could possibly be alive. With the main air crossing into the district destroyed, thus allowing the ventilation to short circuit through to the return, fresh air to disperse the deadly gasses and carry oxygen to the men was not forthcoming. Those miners who had not been killed by the violence of the explosion would soon be overcome by the deadly afterdamp. The work of the rescue teams at the start was exploratory in the hope of finding someone alive. As more rescue teams became available, some of the teams were detailed to recover bodies of victims, but the work of exploration still went on. It came, therefore, as a tremendous surprise when, in the early afternoon of the 16th August, fully 20 hours after the explosion, three miners, J. E. Birkett, D. Hinde and J. J. Weighman, suddenly made their appearance in the main haulage road. They would bring with them the grim news of all the dead bodies that they passed, as they made their way outbye from Skelly's Heading.

On the Friday night the sound of the pit horn brought the people of Whitehaven flocking to the pit head. Within an hour of the news of the explosion having taken place, the road leading to William Pit was lined with hundreds of people. They crowded as near to the gates as the police would allow, and hundreds more gathered on the brows overlooking the pit yard and the winding gear.

The Long Wait, 1947

A group of onlookers gather on the cliff overlooking William Pit, awaiting news of any further developments regarding the rescue/ recovery operations.

The call went out for volunteers and the scene that followed was amazing. Without any thought for their own safety, hundreds of lads and men offered their services and rushed towards the gates that had been opened by the police. Some two hundred were let in and grabbed pit helmets and started work immediately, loading up the timber, brattice cloth and rescue apparatus so vital to the rescue teams underground, who were trying to restore the ventilation in the hope of getting fresh air to the trapped miners.

As the sun went down over the Solway the crowds started to dwindle, leaving behind several hundred men and women who settled down for an all-night vigil. Among them were the wives and mothers of the miners trapped below ground. All through the night the local clergy and the Salvation Army workers moved among the sorrowing relatives giving comfort to those who were now dreading the worst. As the night moved on towards dawn, the miners who understood the dangers of an explosion and it's aftermath were thinking that if no one had walked out of the explosion area by now, there would be little hope of any of them being alive.

By late Saturday afternoon all hope had now been abandoned and the recovery of the bodies would be the priority. Again the call went out for volunteers to remove the 104 bodies from the pit as they were recovered. Once again there was no shortage of men and lads eager to do what they could in this final recovery operation. Some of these volunteers had never worked down a mine, but because they would be carrying the bodies of their father or brother they did not hesitate to come forward. Stories were told of finding miners with their arms clasped around each other as if to give comfort to a marra as they died. Some had been crying, knowing that death was near, the tears washing the coal dust from their cheeks.

The recovery operations continued until the last body was found and arrived at the pit top at 9 p.m. on Saturday the 23rd August 1947. The final call for volunteers was made when it was realised the grave diggers at the local cemeteries could not possibly cope the with the numbers to be buried. Without hesitation they stepped forward again to dig the last resting place for their pit marras.

The Inquiry was held in the Methodist Church Schoolroom, Whitehaven, from the 7th to the 10th October, 1947, and was conducted by Mr. A. M. Bryan, H. M. Chief Inspector of Mines. Some forty-six witnesses were called, and the evidence of the three survivors received nation-wide press coverage. Mr. Abe Moffat of the National Union of Mineworkers called them "The three living miracles". Each told of his own unique experience. On the day of the explosion, Birkett and Hind, both Brushers, descended the pit at 2.30 p.m., while Weighman, a Pan-Puller, descended at 1.30. p.m. They were at their work in the No. 2 Rise District when the explosion occurred.

The Three Survivors of the 1947 Disaster
Left to right - James Weighman, John Birkett and Daniel Hinde.
This picture appeared in the magazine "Illustrated" on 6th September, 1947

Mr. R. J. Edwards, H.M. Divisional Inspector of Mines, examined one of the survivors, Mr. John Birkett. The following evidence given by Birkett was taken from the transcript of that examination.

Q.-You were on this job about 5.30 or just after ?

A.-Yes.

Q.-What happened at the time ?

A.-There was twelve of us together working round where I was, and there was a terrible report.

Q.-One ?

A.-One.

Q.-Yes.?.....

A.-Just as if the drums of our ears had burst, it was that severe, and the air like fluttered, and when it was over everyone said they thought the drums of their ears were going to burst. A chap called Clark, and Hewer, the acting overman, thought that the short wall face had collapsed. So Clark says "Come on, we will go and see Joe", he said "we will go and see if it has collapsed". So they went away, and two or three minutes after I says "I will go and get my bait" but when I got about ten yards up the face someone shouts "Hurry up, come on". When we got up and off the face into the mothergate, we put our clothes on and at the four road ends we were all congregating there when I heard Clark say to Hewer "Hurry up Joe, and get on the face and see what is wrong". Nicholson, the deputy, says "Are we all here?" I said "Yes", and he says "Follow me". We set off to go out. When we got so far by one dip air crossing just up there it was terrible thick, and the deputy started to go down and one or two more, and as he was going down someone asked for an oil lamp. I asked him if he had put his out or had it gone out, and he said he put it out. Then an oil lamp came into my hands, where from I don't know. With that someone says "This door is open". It was the one in the air crossing, and was a very small door. The men started to go in it. Of course being very small, at that time you would have thought they were crushing - they were a shade - and I turned and said , "Don't panic men". When we got in it was red hot. I took my coat off and threw it away, and next thing was Jimmy Rigg says "Can we not get down here Jack?" meaning going down the tailgate and along one dip face and out by the mothergate, and get out. I says "No, we are going to face it all the way".

With that I says to Hinde "Can you tell me where there is any water?" and he says "Main end". I says "Come on in here..."*

Q.-Meaning Skelly's Heading ?

A.-Yes. Skelly's Heading. As I was going I asked a chap to come, but someone shouted to him and he didn't. Why we will never know. As Hinde and I were going down into the end we heard Weighman's voice. He asked if that was Jack, and I said "Yes and Danny". As we were crawling down I says to Hinde "I am not going to make it". He said "Try Jack". I says "I am not going to make it", so he shouted to Weighman and they came and pulled me out down by the loader end into the heading. I laid face down for a long time. When my heart became normal and my head had stopped throbbing I said to Hinde and Weighman, "God is good, we will get out of here". I asked them what water we had, they said two bottles. I said "Don't drink it". I saw what bait I had and had a little bit. They had theirs and after the bait they said "What about having a go?" I says to Weighman "You take the lamp, Jimmy". I had the ....

* *When Birkett asked Hinde for the whereabouts of water, it was not for the purpose of drinking. At 51 years, Birkett was an old experienced miner, and it was always an old mining belief that if there was water in a Heading there would be oxygen that was given off from the water.*

Q.-You are referring to the oil lamp ?

A.-Yes. I says "You take the oil lamp". I had a hawk, and I said "Danny, bring the water, the two bottles". So we tried. When we got about 20 or 30 yard from the inbye side of one dip air crossing we had to retreat back to the heading. We went back and tried two or three times.

Q.-Was the atmosphere stuffy ?

A.-Yes, it was bad.

Q.-It was smokey ?

A.-It was bad. When we were lying, I do not know what time it would be, Hinde says "They are a long time coming Jack", and I said "Yes", but he said "There must be a big fall". I said "There must be". I said "If they have to come from the pit bottom they will hurry, and we will get out as fast as possible". I said "God is good and we will get out". While we were lying there Hinde says "Jack look at this lamp". I looked and gas was right up the barrel, so we decided to have another go. We set off again and when we got to the brow top the lamp went out. He says to me "What are we going to do?" I said "If we go back in there we have had it". I said "If we go on we have a chance of getting out or else we go under". I had a scarf round my neck, and asked Hinde to wet it, which he did. I asked them if they had a scarf and they said "No". I said "Take a stocking off", and Hinde tore his shirt, and Weighman took his vest off. We wet them and set off out. As we were passing the dead, Weighman felt one of their arms, but before we went I said to Jimmy "Take Nicky's oil lamp". We got that oil lamp and we got out to the second air crossing.

Q.-That is the second oil lamp ?

A.-Yes. We got to the crossing and when we got on the top Hinde said "There is a light here", and I said "We don't want that" and then Hinde said "There is air coming up here."
I said "That is where we want to be". As we were going down Hinde said "This is better than winning the Irish Sweep".

The three survivors were met by Bob Brannon the Secretary/Treasurer of the William Pit Miners Lodge, who was working with his repair team timbering up on the next to the last big fall. One of the team thought he saw a shadow inbye the fall. Bob told him that he was dreaming and had been down the pit too long. However he insisted that he saw a shadow and Bob went to investigate and saw it was a shadow coming from approaching lamps. He thought immediately that it was another rescue team that had worked its way inbye via the return airway, and was making its way outbye. He shouted to inquire which rescue team it was. A voice shouted back "Is that Bob Brannon? Thank God there is a God in heaven". It was John Birkett who had shouted and with him were Hinde and Weighman. Bob and his team then helped them to the pit top.

There can be no doubt that it had been a miraculous escape. When the group of miners walked from the faces in No 2 Rise District, little did they know that No 3 main air crossing serving that district had been wrecked and fresh air was not being carried into the district. By the time they reached the air crossing at the junction of No 1 Dip Tailgate and No 3 Trunk Intake, some of them were already being affected by the afterdamp. The timing of Birkett and Hinde leaving the other men was crucial. They walked back inbye to Skelly's Heading. The distance was little more than one hundred yards and Birkett only just made it - he was experiencing the first symptoms of carbon monoxide poisoning. Had it not been for Weighman, who was already in the bottom of Skelly's Heading, coming out to help Hinde drag him down into the heading, he might not have made it. In the short time it took for them to get to the heading, those left at the crossing would in all probability be in the first stages of carbon monoxide poisoning and all would be dead shortly afterwards. (The coroner's reports would subsequently reveal that blood samples from the corpses had a carbon monoxide content of 60%).

Once they reached Skelly's Heading, luck was again on their side. Because the heading inclined inbye and there was no air current to carry the afterdamp into it, there remained sufficient oxygen to support them for a period of time. Also, because of the incline, the methane gas that was being given off accumulated in the roof and moved upwards towards the entrance to the drift. Each time they tried to leave the heading they were forced back by the afterdamp.

By Saturday morning the rescue teams had repaired the air crossings sufficiently to allow fresh air to move inbye, so clearing the afterdamp. Also by Saturday morning the methane in Skelly's heading was increasing in volume and was starting to build up in the heading. It was when Hinde remarked to Birkett that "the gas was right up the barrel" that they decided to move. The wetting of the scarves or vests in order to protect them from the afterdamp, if true, was irrelevant. The wet cloth might help filter dust and smoke, but it could not filter out afterdamp. To reach safety they had to walk several hundred yards along the intake airway inhaling the mine air, and if afterdamp had been present they would have died, as did 90 of the 104 victims. In fact, they were talking to each other as they reached the air crossing where the bodies of 30 victims of afterdamp lay. This was only 130 yards from where they had been waiting at Skelly's Heading. The air was now clear and they walked past many more bodies before meeting with Bob Brannon and his team.

At the inquiry, there was complete agreement as as to the place of origin and the cause of the explosion. The expert witnesses were unanimous that :

(a) The explosion started on No. 2 Dip Longwall Face;

(b) It originated with the firing of a charge of sheathed permitted explosive placed in a rising shot-hole, drilled in the roof between the coal face and the waste, and directed towards the waste;

(c) The shot-hole passed through a roof break, and the inner end of the shot-hole either made contact with, or was in very close proximinity to, a bed-separation cavity;

(d) This cavity contained an accumulation of inflammable gas which was continuous with a larger accumulation of explosive gas in the waste;

(e) The firing of the shot ignited the gas in the bed seperation cavity and the gas burned for a short interval of time before the flame reached the larger accumulation of gas which exploded violently; and

(f) The explosion, once started, traversed a considerable area of working faces and roadways before it was finally arrested, due to a lack of fuel, a considerable distance from the point of origin.

With the exception of the two coal faces in the the district where Birkett, Hinde, and Weighman were working, also Skelly's Heading and the No. 1 Dip Face off No. 3 trunk Road, the explosion traversed almost all other inbye working faces and roadways, and continued outbye along the main return airway for a distance of 60 yards beyond the main air-crossing over No. 3 Trunk Road, and along the main intake haulage road for a distance of approximately 800 yards from its junction with No. 3 Trunk road.

In all, not less than 2,000 yards of roadway were traversed by the flame of the explosion leaving a trail of death and destruction. Almost half of the miners would suffer from burns, some severely, but it was the afterdamp that claimed almost 90% of the victims.

Finally, in his summing up on behalf of the National Coal Board, Mr. Paul E Sandlands, K.C., stated:

"There was a break in No. 3 Shot-hole which should have been detected. It had been suggested that there might have been more air circulating on the face but no amount of air would have prevented this explosion. It was however agreed that the system of ventilation could and should be improved before development went further.

With regard to blame, there was nothing in the evidence to fix the blame on one person or any system."

THE VICTIMS

LEGEND -U/M = Unmarried; W= Widow, followed by number of children.

Name	Age	Address	Dependants
Andrew Agnew	36	17 Todhunters Buildings, Queen St	W/2
Thomas Allan	33	26 Buttermere Ave. Seacliffe	W/2
Harry T Allan	39	45 Hill Top Rd Arrowthwaite	W/2
John Allan	59	5 Buttermere Ave Seacliffe	W/1
John Anderson	50	28 Buttermere Ave Seacliffe	W/6
James Atkinson	45	4 Gameriggs Rd Greenbank	W/4
Richard Atkinson	28	Lady Pit Cottages Whitehaven	W/0
Henry Barker	34	4 Ehen Rd Cleator Moor	W/5
James R Barwise	49	5 Low Harras Moor Whitehaven	W/2
James M Bowes	34	5 Garfield Place Parton	W/3
Thomas Brannon	57	55 Haig Ave Bransty	W/4
Joseph Brannon	45	21 Greenbank Ave Greenbank	W/3
Jacob E Bridges	37	85 Grasmere Ave Woodhouse	W/3
Hartley Byers	35	15 James St Frizington	W/4
Herbert Calvin	40	67 Peter St Whitehaven	W/3
James Campbell	40	81 Woodhouse Rd Woodhouse	W/1
Harold J Carr	22	9 Jane St Frizington	U/M
Richard Cartmell	25	59 Valley View Rd Greenbank	U/M
William Clark	46	15 The Square Parton	W/1
James Clifford	26	72 Frizington Rd Frizington	W/2
Robert Conkey	43	29 Smithfield Egremont	W/2
William H Crofts	45	111 Queen St Whitehaven	W/4
Samuel Devlin	27	9 Union Buildings Low Rd W/n.	W/2
Joseph C Diamond	33	8 Grasmere Ave Woodhouse W/n	W/4
Thomas G Dixon	55	23 Yeathouse Rd Frizington	W/3
John H Doran	50	8 Low Harras Moor Whitehaven	W/8
Wilfred Farrer	34	66 Windermere Rd Woodhouse W/n	W/2

William Fisher	39	12 Gores Buildings Whitehaven	W/4
Thomas Fox	24	29 Bowness Rd Greenbank W/n.	U/M
Joseph Fox	35	11 Woodhouse Rd Woodhouse W/n	U/M
John N Garner	37	41 Frizington Rd Frizington	W/2
James Gibbons	47	60 Seven Acres Parton	U/M
Henry Gibson	36	17 Foundry Rd Parton	W/3
Edward Glaister	48	14 Windermere Rd Woodhouse W/n	W/9
*Robert M Glosson	39	67 Windermere Rd Woodhouse W/n	W/5
Richard E Grearson	47	173 Main St Parton	W/6
William F Grearson	36	96 Main St Parton	W/5

Digging Graves for Victims, 1947

Because the local grave-diggers could not cope with the sudden huge demand for graves, many miners immediately volunteered to dig the last resting place for their pit marras.

Joseph W Hewer	40	18a Seven Acres Parton	W/5
Ronald W Hewer	38	110 Main St Parton	W/4
Ronald Hughes	20	Hospital House Bransty W/n.	U/M
George Hutchinson	44	7 James Pit Whitehaven	W/1
William Johnson	27	43 Trumpet Rd Cleator Moor	W/2
George Johnston	41	38 Lakeland Ave Seacliffe W/n.	W/3
James W Lambert	35	1 Plumblands Lane Whitehaven	W/2
Thomas Lancaster	27	33 Basket Rd Arrowthwaite Kells	U/M
William H Lee	27	29 Aldby St Cleator Moor	W/0

* *Note; Robert M. Glosson was better known as Robert (Bob) Mullholland*

James Leeson	48	10 Dyke St Frizington	U/M
Dennis Lyons	31	4 Lakeland Ave Seacliffe W/n.	U/M
John H Maddison	22	72 Fell View Ave Woodhouse W/n.	W/2
Joseph B Marshall	48	70 George St Whitehaven	Widower/2
William Martin	32	3 Wellington Row Whitehaven	W/2
Edward McAllister	24	Sun Inn Parton	W/2
Isaac McAllister	54	15 Benticks Row Ginns W/n.	W/8
James McMullen	27	16a Sandhills Lane Whitehaven	W/2
William T McMullen	23	20a Roper St Whitehaven	W/1
Vincent McSherry	37	2 Crummock Ave Woodhouse W/n.	W/2
John Milburn	40	94 Grasmere Ave Woodhouse W/n.	W/2
John E Moore	37	3 John Sq. Peter St Whitehaven	W/3
James Moore	63	96b George St Whitehaven	W/2
Joseph Moore	46	64 Seven Acres Parton	W/3
John R Mowat	26	3 Lowther St Whitehaven	W/1
Francis Murdock	38	11 Todhunters Blds Queen St W/n.	W/3
James Murray	36	22 Crummock Ave Woodhouse W/n	W/4
William Murray	39	5 Lady Pit Terr Sunny Hill W/n	W/3
Lawrence H P Murtagh	41	73 Buttermere Ave Seacliffe W/n.	W/3
Patrick Murtagh	28	Old Woodhouse Whitehaven	W/2
William R Musson	22	The Rose and Thistle West Strand	W/0
Richard Musson	36	22 Brisco Crescent Parton	U/M
Thomas Nelson	36	Summer Grove Cottages Hensingham	W/3
William Nicholson	33	1 Temple Terr Catherine St W/n.	W/1
Joseph Norman	41	1 The Close Bransty Whitehaven	W/3
Sydney O'Fee	34	62 Windermere Rd Woodhouse W/n.	W/3
John A Paragreen	30	9 Bransty Row Bransty	W/0
William L Pickering	24	28 Haig Ave Bransty Whitehaven	W/1
John Pilkington	32	6 Longmires Court Queen St W/n.	W/4
William Pilkington	66	60 Windermere Rd Woodhouse W/n.	W/5
William Pilkington	51	21 Woodhouse Rd Woodhouse W/n.	W/0
Thomas Pilkington	27	60 Windermere Rd Woodhouse W/n.	U/M
George Porthouse	54	16 North Rd Bransty	W/grown up family
John Quirk	38	23 Victoria Road Whitehaven	W/1
Adam Raby	26	45 Fleswick Ave Woodhouse W/n.	W/0
Edward R Ray	31	1 Front Row Northside Workington	W/1
John J Renwick	39	12 Gameriggs Rd Greenbank W/n.	W/2
Thomas Richardson	40	150 Queen St Whitehaven	W/0
James Rigg	28	12 Marlborough St Whitehaven	W/1
John Robbs	56	6 Brayton Rd Bransty Whitehaven	W/9
Albert E Saulters	40	12 Meadow View Castle Croft Egmt.	W/1
Leonard Seward	36	7 Pasture Rd Rowrah	W/2

Thomas Shackley	40	76 Low Church St Whitehaven	U/M
Mark J Shaw	45	30 North Rd Bransty Whitehaven	W/7
Henry Shilton	44	23 Main St Parton	W/0
Thomas B Smith	62	2 Torrentines Blds Tangier St W/n.	W/3
Thomas T Smith	32	7 South Row Kells Whitehaven	W/3
Harold Smith	41	31 Solway Rd Moresby Parks	W/0
Thomas Turner	46	17 George St Whitehaven	W/1
Albert Tweddle	31	6 Fleswick Ave Woodhouse W/n	W/0
William A Walby	46	The Lodge Ewanrigg Hall Maryport	W/0
Ralph Walker	34	16 Valley View Rd Greenbank W/n.	W/2
William Williamson	27	14 Hilton Terr Whitehaven	W/1
George H Wilson	29	Douglas Burn Mkt Place Whitehaven	W/1
Matthew Wilson	46	27 South Row Kells Whitehaven	U/M
Joseph Wilson	38	72 Valley View Rd Greenbank W/n.	W/2
Thomas Woodend	64	11 South View Rd Bransty W/n	W/0
Walter Wylie	26	36 Fell View Ave Woodhouse W/n.	W/2

Chapter 14

Survivors of Explosions

There are not many miners living today who have experienced and survived an underground explosion. Usually any miners on the inbye side of the explosion are killed as a result of the violence of the blast or from Carbon Monoxide poisoning, (afterdamp). In the Wellington Pit Disaster in 1910, and with the exception of two who walked out past the fire, all those miners who survived the explosion itself, died as a result of being on the inbye side of the fire that was started by the explosion. In the William Pit explosion of 1947, 90 of the 104 victims were killed by the afterdamp. Only three would walk to freedom.

This chapter deals with three miners who were in the William Pit when it exploded, and lived to tell the tale.

Moses Stephens

Moses Stephens was born in Bardy Lane on the West Strand, Whitehaven, on the 12th February 1924. In 1934 as part of a slum clearance scheme, all the inhabitants of that area including Mount Pleasant, were moved to the new Woodhouse Estate. Moses lived at No 50, Fell View Avenue, next door to his marra James George. Together they started work at Haig Pit, working on the pit top, but before very long they decided to move to William Pit. There they were employed at the pit bottom pulling the empty tubs from the cage and preparing them to be made into sets to be sent inbye.

They were later moved inbye to work on the haulage roads in the Countess Bannock District. Their job was at the bottom of No 2 Dip, sending the full tubs of coal from No 2 Dip Face up to the Countess Bannock Main Haulage Road. There the tubs were transferred by two other haulage hands onto the main haulage rope to be sent outbye to the pit bottom. From there the tubs were sent to the surface through the downcast shaft.

On Tuesday, 3rd June, 1941, Moses (17) and James George (18), left home together to work on the back shift. Moses recalls that the district was sweltering hot that day, and thought that they should not have been sent in there. Because there was a shortage of haulage hands due to absenteeism, instead of working at the bottom of No 2 dip doing their usual job, they were told to work at the top, transferring the tubs onto the main rope. The main haulage rope was "Overhead Haulage": instead of running along the floor of the roadway on rollers, it was held near the roof of the roadway by pulleys. The tubs were secured to the rope by an Automatic Lever Clip, better known as the "Hambone" Clip . This transfer from their usual job to the entrance to the dip would result in the death of James and serious injuries to Moses.

At about 2.15 p.m. Moses and James were standing outside the entrance to No 2 dip waiting for full tubs to come up the dip. All that Moses can remember is that he was facing inbye when he felt as if a hurricane had suddenly developed which picked him up and hurled him off his feet. It seemed to pick him up again and as he passed out he felt something pinning him to the ground. What happened after Moses became unconscious, was told to him by his rescuers at a later date. The force of the explosion had lifted the haulage rope off the pulleys whilst it was still running, it struck Moses and James George and pinned them to the ground almost severing Moses right arm above the elbow and fatally injuring James.

When the rescuers arrived on the scene the rope had been stopped and they were released from underneath it. The rescuers thought that Moses was dead and placed him to one side in a manhole. A rescuer named Jinky Corkhill took another look at Moses and held the glass face of his pocket watch to the mouth of Moses and realised that he was still breathing. He called to the other rescuers and Moses was put on a stretcher and carried outbye to the shaft. The rescuers had to climb over the hot and overturned tubs at Lowca Junction.

Moses recovered consciousness next day to find himself in the Whitehaven Hospital, where his right arm had been amputated above the elbow. He also had head and face injuries and was burned on his legs. These injuries put an end to what would have been a very promising sporting career. In 1939 aged 15, Moses was the Cumberland and Westmorland 7st 71bs Boxing Champion, and he recalls as one of his greatest sporting moments when as a member of the Kells Boys Club Cross Country Team they beat St Bees Grammar School.

No one told Moses that his "Best Marra" had been killed in the explosion. He only found out when he saw the Whitehaven News with all the names of the dead. Moses faintly remembers struggling to get out of bed to try to get home, but he collapsed at the bottom of some stairs and remembered nothing further until next day. It was to be three weeks before Moses was released from hospital and he was still in bandages when called to give evidence at the inquiry into the disaster on Tuesday 29th July 1941. He recalls that it was quite an ordeal for a seventeen year old to be put through a session of questioning by some very important and prominent members of the Coal Industry.

Moses never went underground again. When he had recovered from his injuries and amputation he was given a job on the pit top in the stores at William Pit. He left the Coal Mining Industry and was later employed at the Royal Ordinance Factory at Sellafield on the Telephone Exchange. He then moved to the West Cumberland Hospital in the same capacity, where he remained for 29 years before retiring through ill health. Now 73, he lives with his daughter Eleanor at 31 Gable Road Mirehouse.

Lawrence (Larry) McCormick

The son of John McCormick, a miner who worked at Walkmill Pit, Larry McCormick was born on the 9th April 1911, on the Middle Row, Newhouses. He was one of a family of six, having one sister and four brothers. He attended Quay Street and St Beghs schools until he was 14 years old, leaving school in 1925 and starting work at Ladysmith Pit the following week.

His first job was operating a pump which was pumping water out of the pit. Later he was employed on the haulage roads sending the full tubs of coal outbye to the shaft, and the empty tubs inbye to the working headings. By the time he was twenty he was hewing coals in the Main Band Seam which was about nine feet high They used 9 ft wooden props to support the huge 'cross heads', (wooden beams) which supported the roof. The face was worked by teams of three men, Larry, his older brother John, and 'Dougie' Amor forming one of these teams. Two would do the hewing and one would do the trailing. There were no compressed air picks in those days recalls Larry. They would "lay in" with hand picks. This was done by laying on the floor on their sides, and cutting the coal out from the bottom of the seam to a depth of four or five feet. To protect themselves against the coal falling on top of them, short blocks of wood (sprags) were set behind the hewer to support the coal as he "laid in". Once they had cut out sufficient coals, holes would be bored into the coal using a hand operated boring machine and the Shot Firer would then blast the coals down.

As the hewers filled the tubs the trailer would push the full tubs to the haulage road, a distance of about 50 yards, where they were turned on a flat sheet and pushed into a siding ready to be sent outbye. The team never stopped for 'bait', each man in turn would eat his food as the other two worked. Each tub had a small curled hook welded to the rear of the tub commonly known as the "pig's tail". Each team of men had a set of tokens with their own name or allotted number stamped onto them. These would be hooked onto the pig's tail to identify which team the coals belong to, when weighed by the weighman and the union check weighman on the pit top. This was before cap-lamps were available, and miners were issued with clumsy hand lamps. As each man walked along carrying his tools and bait, the lamp was hooked onto the front of his belt and bumped against his knees.

Larry remembered all too well the bath time at home in the Newhouses. They had no bathroom in those days, nor any running water in the house. On getting home at 7.00 a.m. from the night shift, and before they had their breakfast, his mother, Mary McCormick, would have the tin bath set in front of the fire partly filled with cold water she had collected in buckets from the outside taps. Two large kettles each holding more than a gallon of water would be boiling on the fire. The cold water in the bath was made warm by adding to it the two kettles of boiling water. Larry's mother would say to her two sons "Who is first today?" and the lucky one would have the pleasure of bathing in clean hot water. The other would have to make do with much cooler, dirtier water. The next day, the order was reversed.

Larry worked at Ladysmith until it closed in 1931. He was then transferred to William Pit to work on the coal faces. The method of mining the coals was different at William. Larry worked on Longwall Faces where the coal was undercut by coal cutting machines. Each man was given a "stint" measured out by the Puffler. Each hewer would fill his own coal and set his own supports, on average they would fill ten tons of coals per shift. The faces Larry worked on were only three and a half feet high so he had to work on his knees which were protected by knee pads.

On the day of the explosion on 3rd June 1941, Larry was working on No 2 Dip Face. He knew something had gone wrong when he felt the reversal of the ventilation. The Deputy, Bob Casson, went onto the face and told them that something had gone wrong and to get outbye, warning them not to go into the return airway but by the intake airway. Larry set off with two lads named Scottie Phillips and Joe Williams. When they got to the top of No 2 Dip the air doors were jammed fast so they forced them open with an iron bar. They got to the haulage road of the Countess Bannock intake airway and set off towards Lowca Junction and outbye. They passed the bodies of some dead miners but could not stop because of the fumes and gas. At Lowca Junction they had to climb over the derailed tubs and rubble to get further outbye. On the way out they met the Manager, Mr. Farquhar, and Mr. Dawson, who told them to keep moving towards the pit bottom, this they did and were eventually able to leave the pit. Larry walked home to Woodhouse and to his wife, who had no knowledge of the explosion that had taken place.

Larry was off work for three weeks recovering from the effects of the gas. During this period he received a letter telling him to start at Haig Pit when he was recovered, which was at the end of June 1941. He was first employed as a "brusher", enlarging the intake and return roadways as the Longwall Face advanced. The brushers' usually worked in teams of four, and Larry was given a job with George Skillicorn's team in the Main West Bannock. He later went to work on the coal face and remained in that job until 1968. It was then whilst he was filling coal that a huge lump fell over towards Larry and fractured his right leg.

Larry never went back to face-work. When he recovered from this accident, he was given a job attending to the huge "Booster Fan" in The 4 South District, one of the most powerful in the country. Without this fan Haig Pit would never have been able to ventilate the workings and disperse the methane gas, that was given off as the faces were worked. So vital was the fan to the safe working of the pit, it was attended twenty-four hours a day, seven days a week.

Larry's next and final job was working on No 4 Riding Road. This was the intake airway in which the "Man Riding Train" operated. This train carried the miners for almost 3 miles inbye to the Main West District. In order to ensure the safe running of the train, Larry's task was to keep the track clear of debris, and to maintain the rollers and roller boxes that supported the haulage rope that pulled the train along the roadway.

Larry retired from Haig Pit in 1976 aged 65. He was presented with a framed certificate given by The National Coal Board in recognition of 51 years underground service to the industry. A scant reward to Larry or to all the other old miners who at times were to gamble their lives, winning coal from the bowels of the earth beneath the Solway Firth.

Larry, now 86, lives at 18, Snebro Road, Mirehouse.

Stephen Tyson Ferguson

Stephen Tyson Ferguson, was born on the 8th September, 1919, at 102, Middle Row, Newhouses. He was born into a mining family, having six brothers and four sisters, all of the boys in the family were employed in coal mining. His father and grandfather both worked in William Pit. His grandfather, Henry Tyson, died on Monday 14th January 1895, after being ran over by a set of tubs in William Pit. Mrs Tyson, was one of the three Whitehaven Screen Girls who travelled to London in May 1887, as part of a deputation to protest against the bill to prohibit female labour on the pit screens.

At the age of fourteen, Stephen left school on a Friday in 1933, and started work down William Pit on the Sunday night shift. His first job was driving a haulage engine in the Lowca District. He was still engaged in haulage work when the Whitehaven Collieries closed in October 1935, being under 18 years of age he was not allowed any dole, and had to rely on his parents to keep him until they re-opened again in March 1937.

On Tuesday 3rd of June, 1941, Stephen was working in William Pit when the explosion took place. In his own words he recalls what happened.

"I was on the first shift that day working as a haulage hand at the top of Countess Bannock brow. I had finished my shift and was relieved by my back shift "Marra" John Burney. Dick Glaister who was the Rope Splicer, asked me to stay back and help him to repair a damaged haulage rope. After we had completed the job I made my way outbye to the pit bottom. It was there that I met the Manager Mr. George Farquhar, he told me that there had been an explosion inbye in the vicinity of Lowca Junction.

I returned inbye with the manager and his party, and when we got to the Lowca Junction there was a fire showing behind the stopping wall. There was lots of tubs de-railed and the bodies of three miners were lying in the area. There was ten miners killed that day including my back shift marra John Burney, and two more died as a result of their injuries a few days later bringing the total to twelve. Several others were injured and burnt, Dick Glaister with whom I had been working was one of them and Moses Stephens lost an arm.

The old Countess District had been on fire for years, but several brick stoppings had been built to combat the fires. The pit was closed down for a while and the Countess Bannock district sealed off and never worked again. Coal was mined only from the Six Quarters seam.

After the explosion I joined the Royal Air Force in August of that year."

In 1945 Stephen returned to work in William Pit, first as a haulage hand, then as 'Pan Puller' and later as a Deputy. It was when he was working as a Deputy on the back shift in August 1947, the pit exploded again.

Stephen remembers the events of that fateful day as follows:

"I descended the shaft at one o'clock on Friday the 15th August 1947, as one of the back shift Deputies. At the pit bottom I tested all the back shift men's lamps also carrying out a random search.(Checking to see if any miner is carrying matches or cigarettes) *I then proceeded inbye to a heading, where Joe and Arthur Rutherford were working in the development and found everything in order.*

I then took two men, Joe Fox and Joe Marshall, into the Main Return Airway to a point about a hundred yards inbye that was known as "The Wellington Pit Doors" where I required some repair work done. After giving instructions as to what had to be done, I left them to get on with their work. Then I proceeded outbye in the Main Return to the upcast shaft and from there back onto the Main Intake Road. There I met Fred Smith coming outbye, he said he was going up the pit for a bottle of oil. I then carried on to where the Rutherfords were working, which was also the place where the Deputies' Station was located.

After a short break I started to fill in my mid-shift report and had just entered the time (which was 5.40 p.m.) when the pit exploded. I thought my head was about to burst and when I looked at Joe Rutherford he was holding his head. Arthur who was further outbye near the entrance to the heading, felt it much stronger than we did.

We then decided to make our way to the main road, when we got there we found it very heavy with dust which was travelling inbye. This gave me the impression that something had happened outbye near to the pit bottom. I immediately phoned the pit bottom, but was told by the onsetter everything was all right, but he reported that a gale of wind had come from inbye and nearly blew him over. The dust coming inbye had been lifted by the initial shock wave of the explosion and was being carried back inbye by the ventilation current. I then knew that something very serious had happened inbye from where we were. I then tried to phone inbye but got no response from any of the phones.

I then decided to make my way inbye with Joe Rutherford, telling Arthur to stay by the telephone, so that I could ring him from the next phone inbye to let him know how we were.

When we reached the top of the Six Quarters I could smell the effect of the explosion. My immediate thoughts were for the safety of the two workers I had left in the return airway. I set off with Joe in that direction but when we reached the air doors leading into the return airway, we found that the airway was full of afterdamp, (carbon monoxide) *and we made a hasty retreat closing the doors behind us.*

I then decided to go down into the Six Quarters Seam where we met three men named Allan, Kirven, and McQuire who were slightly injured but able to walk. We went back up from Six Quarters and met Billy Adair. I instructed Billy to make his way outbye with the three casualties and get them safely up the pit. Allan was reluctant to go outbye which was understandable, as he had his son and his brother and two nephews in the explosion area.

Shortly afterwards the manager Mr. McAllister arrived on the scene. I told him about the main return being full of gas, this he confirmed with a quick inspection. At this point we were the only ones in the explosion area. The rescue teams were still on their way to the pit with breathing apparatus, the manager having called them out as soon as he had realised the gravity of the situation.

He then decided to proceed inbye down the Six Quarters District. The two Rutherford brothers (Arthur had now joined us coming inbye after the manager) and myself told him that we were going with him, he thanked us and said that he appreciated what we were doing.

When we reached a place that was known as the Oily Drift it was evident that there had been a violent explosion. On reaching the old No 2 Rise, we found all the devastation caused by the explosion. The girders had been blown out and were all twisted and misplaced resulting in heavy falls of roof and extremely dangerous conditions. We tried to get further inbye over the falls, we got passed two but could get no further and had to retreat because of the foul air.

We rested for a few minutes to clear our lungs and the manager voiced what I had also been thinking, that if there were any survivors they would have been coming out by now. But only three did make it to safety. The following day Daniel Hind, John Birkett, and John Weighman, miraculously walked out of the pit.

The manger then decided to try the Main Return Airway from No 2 Rise, but when we reached it we found the Air Lock doors blown open and fouled by gas. We immediately closed them allowing the ventilation to travel inbye but then we had to retreat because of more falling roof and foul air.

In all 104 miners perished that day including the two I had set to work in the Main Return Airway. I must say that if I have ever met some brave men, I met them on that fateful night of 15 August 1947 - the manager Mr Billy McAllister, and the brothers Joe and Arthur Rutherford."

Stephen Tyson Ferguson continued to work at William until it's closure in December 1954. He was transferred to Haig Pit where he worked as a Pan Puller and later as a Deputy. In 1961 he decided to leave the Coal Industry and was employed at Smith Bros., Whitehaven, until he retired in 1982. Stephen, now 77, lives with his wife Annie, and daughter Pam, at 13, Ashness Close, Mirehouse.

Appendix A

List of Explosions and Disasters

Resulting in loss of life, in the Whitehaven & District Coal Mines

Name of pit	Date	Deaths	Remarks
Priestgill (Hensingham)	1682	1	First recorded explosion
Unknown pits	28 Feb 1752	1	
" "	14 Aug 1753	1	
" "	25 Aug 1753	2	
" "	7 Apr 1754	1	
" "	14 Jun 1754	1	
" "	7 Aug 1755	1	Carlisle Spedding killed* *see note, pg. 137*
" "	7 Jun 1757	1	
" "	29 May 1758	1	
" "	23 Jun 1758	2	
" "	4 Sep 1759	1	
" "	4 Jun 1760	4	
" "	16 May 1769	4	
" "	15 Jan 1772	1	
" "	11 Apr 1773	1	
" "	6 Jan 1775	1	
" "	17 Aug 1775	2	
" "	27 Oct 1775	1	
" "	23 Jan 1776	1	
" "	1 Feb 1776	1	
" "	2 Aug 1779	1	
" "	8 Aug 1781	1	
" "	16 Oct 1781	2	1 man, 1 woman; 2 horses
" "	5 Feb 1785	3	
" "	16 Jun 1785	1	
" "	31 Jan 1791	3	Innundation. 2 men, 1 woman, 5 horses
" "	2 May 1827	1	
" "	26 Mar 1829	1	
" "	1 Jan 1831	1	
" "	29 May 1839	1	
Bottle Bank Pit	June 1819	1	
Cleator Moor Pit	26 Dec 1843	1	
Cleator Moor No. 2 Pit	13 Jul 1852	1	
Cleator Moor New Pit	20 Dec 1857	1	
Corporal	5 Aug 1737	22	21 men, 1 woman; 3 horses
Countess	20 Jan 1841	2	
"	15 Jul 1843	1	
Country	6 Aug 1775	5	

Croft	19 Jul 1822	1	
"	21 Dec 1824	1	
"	6 Aug 1828	5	
"	12 Nov 1831	22	Included four boys
"	20 May 1847	4	
"	28 Jun 1855	5	
"	12 Aug 1858	3	
"	26 Mar 1861	2	
Duke	26 Apr 1842	1	
"	31 Jan 1843	1	
"	11 Jan 1844	11	Plus 11 horses
Frizington	3 Jun 1871	1	
Frizington (Oatlands)	3 Dec 1900	1	
Haig	5 Sept 1922	39	
"	13 Sep 1927	4	
"	12 Feb 1928	13	
"	29 Jan 1931	27	
Hind	1740	2	
Hope	27 Jan 1862	1	
"	21 Jul 1862	2	
Kells	30 Oct 1819	21	
Lamb Hill	11 Apr 1843	1	
Lattera	10 Mar 1700	1	
Lowca No. 9	9 Apr 1883	1	
Lowca No. 10	9 Dec 1946	15	
North	30 May 1826	1	
"	4 Apr 1835	1	
Saltom	27 Feb 1819	5	
"	21 Jun 1824	2	
"	15 Feb 1826	1	
"	25 Jul 1833	1	
"	24 Sep 1842	1	
Scaleby	6 Jan 1775	1	
Scalegill	24 May 1775	1	Plus 3 Burnt
"	8 Aug 1781	1	
Threapthwaite (Arlecdon)	11 Jul 1849	1	
" "	7 Jul 1854	1	
" "	11 Aug 1854	2	
Wellington	18 Feb 1854	1	
"	13 Jun 1858	1	
"	11 May 1910	136	Worst disaster in Cumbrian coalfield
"	6 Dec 1920	3	
Whinney Hill	28 Oct 1848	30	
William	28 Apr 1810	2	Plus four burnt
"	13 Apr 1821	12	Including 3 boys & 4 girls
"	13 Oct 1823	32	Including 15 boys, 2 girls & 17 horses
"	2 Jan 1826	9	Suffocated by underground fire
"	18 Mar 1828	1	
"	6 Feb 1830	3	Three boys
"	18 Feb 1839	23	Including nine boys

"	30 Sept 1842	1	
"	17 Dec 1847	1	
"	12 Mar 1850	2	
"	25 Apr 1882	4	
"	26 Nov 1907	5	
"	11 Jul 1922	2	
"	3 Jun 1941	12	Explosion of water gas
"	15 Aug 1947	104	
Wilson	23 Feb 1779	5	Including 4 women & 4 horses
"	Nov 1835	1	A woman
Wreay	3 Aug 1846	2	
Wyndham	8 Feb 1845	2	
"	19 Mar 1847	1	

Note: *Carlisle Spedding was buried at Holy Trinity Church on 10th August 1755, but the pit in which he was killed is not recorded. It seems likely that he met his death around the 6th August 1755 at Country Pit, along with five other men.*

List of Adults Killed in William Pit
(*Excluding* Explosions of Firedamp)

Name	Age	Date	Type of Accident
Thomas Askew	50	17.03.1883	?
Lawrence Baily	?	10.04.1837	Run over by waggons
William Birney	17	26.08.1867	Run over by tubs
James Ramsay Bradley	35	18.06.1908	Struck by girder
Joseph Brannon	43	17.09.1946	Roof fall
William Bridson	?	04.03.1840	Roof fall
William HR Briggs	39	17.05.1938	Roof fall
Thomas Bulman	16	06.09 1831	Driver; kicked by horse
Edward Burns	39	15.11.1916	Roof fall
James Byrne	?	27.12.1833	Roof fall
William Campbell	35	21.08.1849	Crushed by waggons
Ernest Chalmers	16	09.01.1904	Roof fall
Edward Christopher	35	20.01.1951	Roof fall
John Clark	20	10.08.1833	Fell down shaft
Thomas Corlett	32	03.07.1878	Shot firing
John Dailey	16	07.07.1875	Crushed by cage
William Davys	16	04.10.1845	Roof fall
Patrick Denvar	?	19.09.1848	Crushed by baskets
John Dixon	60	29.12.1835	Fell down shaft
John Dixon	31	01.08.1944	Shot firing injury
Thomas Holliday Dixon	38	15.05.1906	Died in pit (?)
Edward Doran	49	08.11.1845	Roof fall
John Doran	66	23.10 1895	Run over by tubs
William Doran	52	26.05.1900	Crushed by side coal
James Doughty	44	12.05.1919	Roof fall
Barrow Dryden	53	07.07.1849	Fell down shaft
James Dunn	55	24.08.1877	Fell onto head at pit top
William Egram	54	05.06.1874	Crushed by arch
Thomas Eavans	23	11.04.1911	Roof fall
William Evans	42	15.06.1902	Roof fall
Michael Ferguson	54	19.03.1924	Run over by tubs
William Fitzsimmons	33	21.04.1911	Blood poisoning from crushed hand
John Flinn	46	31.03.1854	Roof fall
Michael Joseph Fowler	43	31.03.1917	Died from injuries sustained in April, 1916
Henry Garrity	32	21.01 1907	Run over by tubs
Anthony Graham	15	06.06.1839	Run over by waggon at pit top
John Hadwin	21	21.05.1823	Roof fall
Lancelot Haggan	57	13.01.1865	Fall of top coal
William Hall	16	24.01.1942	Struck by prop
Thomas Harling	35	29.07.1819	Roof fall

Richard Hornsby	66	18.08.1913	Roof fall
Thomas Horrocks	27	19.03.1903	Roof fall
Hugh Hughes	41	02.07.1903	Roof fall
Henry Johnston	?	30.10.1833	Roof fall
Thomas Johnson	32	29.02.1883	Run over by waggons on pit top
Patrick Kinsella	17	03.03.1900	Driver; kicked by horse
Bernard Lundy	?	? 01.1850	Scalded at Fire Engine
William Lundy	17	23 09.1861	Run over by trams
Peter McAllister	24	20.09.1842	Fell from basket
Matthew McCall	44	09.04.1884	Run over by tubs
John McClusky	62	13.03.1916	Roof fall
John McCully	18	15.03.1875	Run over by waggons on pit top
John McGarry	63	24.07.1852	Roof fall
William McGill	41	05.03.1840	Crushed by side coal
James McGuire	47	02.10.1830	Roof fall
John McGuire (son of James)	17	31.05.1832	Fell from basket
Isaac McIntyre	21	23.02.1927	Run over by tubs
James McKitten	30	05.10.1848	Roof fall
Thomas McLaughlin	30	09.01.1893	Shot firing
William McLaughlin	68	11.09.1931	Fell 60ft. on pit top
Hugh McMillan	53	03.08.1854	Roof fall
James Mason	26	11.03.1829	Fell down shaft
William Matthews	66	04.04.1855	Roof fall
Mathew Mickin	?	16.10.1839	Fell from basket
Thomas Millar	19	31.10.1882	Crushed by waggons on pit top
Michael Morgan	86	20 11.1853	Fell from basket
Dixon Mossop	34	05.06.1874	Crushed by arch
John Mossop	23	19.03.1903	Roof fall
Daniel Nicholson	54	07.07.1954	Died in pit (?)
William Parkinson	17	16.07.1909	Crushed by tubs
Roland Pritchard	48	26.04.1932	Roof fall
James Quayle	56	10.10.1890	Roof fall
John Quayle	26	13.05.1841	Roof fall
Thomas Quayle	47	25.12.1917	Fractured skull
Richard M Richardson	35	14.07.1941	Roof fall
William Robbs	28	24.08.1922	Roof fall
Francis Roney	16	12.08.1886	Crushed by trams
Isaac Rothery	63	30.04.1930	Roof fall
Charles Sayle	61	08.12.1909	Injured on screens
John C Shepherd	53	13.07.1943	Roof fall
Alfred Skelly	52	14.05.1920	Roof fall
Hugh Smith	18	07.01.1861	Crushed between bogie & girder
John Smith	?	26.12.1835	Fell down shaft
Thomas Smith	45	? 09 1829	Roof fall
William Spence	73	18.08.1903	Run over by set
Joseph Stephenson	30	19.11.1917	Roof fall
William Tate	45	07.02.1878	Roof fall
William Telford	41	02.10.1917	Roof fall
John Thompson	66	06.07 1938	Roof fall
John Thornton	33	03.07.1856	Roof fall

Frederick Thwaites	38	16.09.1940	Roof fall
William Tinkler	23	04.04.1848	Roof fall
Jos Topping	45	12.01.1849	Fell down shaft
Matthew Trembath	57	12.04.1944	Run over by tubs
Henry Turner	24	26.02.1853	Hooker; struck by coals falling from basket
John Tyrell	30	05.02.1835	Fell from basket
Henry Tyson	34	16.01.1895	Run over by tubs
Elisha Vickers	37	? 03 1834	Killed by sack of oats falling down shaft
(?) Waters	?	21.11.1831	Roof fall
William Watson	65	12.07.1875	Crushed by baskets
William Watson	53	16.111937	Roof fall
William Whineray	26	18.06.1900	Roof fall
Robert Wilkinson	35	23.11.1917	Roof fall
Frank Williamson	26	08.05.1913	Crushed by waggons on pit top
James Henry Wilson	50	20.06.1933	Roof fall
John Wren	54	14.09.1854	Killed whilst "laying in"

Appendix C

List of Children Under Fifteen Years Old Killed in William Pit

Note: the names of those killed by ***explosions or fire*** also appear in the relevant accounts of disasters (See Chapter 13)

Name	Age	Date	Cause of Death
William Atkinson	14	18.02.1839	Explosion of firedamp
Matthew Blaylock	14	13.10.1823	"
Ann Bainbridge	11	13.10.1823	"
Richard Cousins	14	18.03.1828	"
Joseph Clark	14	18.02.1839	"
John Cowan	13	10.11.1887	Run over by bogies
James Downie	14	06.02.1830	Explosion of firedamp
William Dornan	14	18.02.1839	"
John Dunn	11	18.02.1839	"
John Fisher	10	18.02.1839	"
Thomas Flood	13	03.01.1826	Suffocated by fire
Thomas Gardiner	10	05.06.1839	Run over by waggons
John Gill	11	13.04.1821	Explosion of firedamp
Peter Gribbin	14	13.11.1868	Crushed by rolley train
John Herring	14	13.10.1823	Explosion of firedamp
George McAllister	13	04.06.1861	Kicked by horse
John McLellon	13	13.10.1823	Explosion of firedamp
William McMullen	11	18.02.1839	"
Charles Morgan	14	17.04.1874	Crushed by baskets
Patrick Murray	14	17.08.1900	Run over by tubs
Christopher Pearson	14	18.02.1839	Explosion of firedamp
Thomas Shields	12	06.02.1830	"
Robert Tear	12	18.02.1839	"
Thomas Watson	13	15.08.1884	Crushed under cage
Michael Wheatly	13	18.02.1839	Explosion of firedamp
Issac Williamson	12	17.06.1847	Fell down shaft

Appendix D

CHILDREN'S EMPLOYMENT COMMISSION FIRST REPORT OF THE COMMISSIONERS

This report was first published in 1842, and deals with the inquiry into the employment of Females, Children and Young Persons in mines in Great Britain.

In 1841, Mr. J. C. Symons, one of the Sub Commissioners, visited Cumberland and in particular the William Pit at Whitehaven. The text of his report is given in full, as it provides an unbiased account by a person from outside the County and the Coal Mining Industry, of the conditions that prevailed in the Whitehaven pits at that time.

THE CUMBERLAND COAL MINES

Report

By Jellinger C. Symons, Esq., on the Employment of Children and Young Persons in Mines of the Cumberland Coal Field; and on State, Condition, and Treatment of such Children and Young Persons.

TO HER MAJESTY'S COMMISSIONERS.

London. August 12. 1841.

Gentlemen,

1. The fortnight allowed to me for a rapid investigation of the Cumberland Collieries has enabled me to report merely on the prominent features of the condition of those who are the subject of our inquiry. I found evidence in some cases difficult to obtain, owing to the extreme fear of offending great men, on the part of timid or dependent witnesses.

2. The children do not begin to work in the Cumberland Collieries so early as in Yorkshire; for the coal seams are all of a good thickness; in the inland collieries they are at least four or five feet thick, and in the sea coast ones eight, nine and ten feet thick. Ten years is the common age for children to begin work; and they seldom commence before eight and a half years of age.

3. I can find no correct estimate of the children who work in the Cumberland Pits. (See appendix B for the William Pit children) They certainly are not so numerous, even in proportion to the men, as in Yorkshire.

4. This is chiefly owing to the far greater use of horses for conveying the coals from the foreheads (banks) to the shaft. In all Lord Lonsdale's collieries, and in fact, generally on the coast of Cumberland, no lads or children are employed in trailing, putting, or hurrying. The coal is all worked out on the Newcastle plan, which it is of course needless to describe to you, (the Bord and Pillar System) and this, together with the height of the coal seams, admits of the horses being brought up to the workings, thence drawing the corves or baskets away.

5. Boys and lads are consequently employed to drive the trams of baskets or corves, of which several are hooked together, along the tram-ways. These journeys are greatly lengthened owing to many of the large collieries being submarine. In the William Pit they have 500 acres under the sea, and the distance is two and a half miles from the shaft to the extreme part of the workings. There is a stable also under the sea, in this immense pit, for forty-five horses. The shaft is 110 fathoms.

6. And here I must state that a feature exists in this driving employment I have not hitherto seen, and which constitutes the chief labour of the occupation. To prevent the basket from running down hill and falling on the heels of the horses, it is customary for the driver to place himself as a post between the foremost basket and the buttocks of the horse. He places his left shoulder against the horse, the right foot on the rail of the tram, and the right hand on the top of the basket; the left leg being generally supported by the trace. When the train of corves is heavily laden, or the descent very steep, a pole (locking) is placed through the hind wheels of the trams, and thus it is in a measure dragged. Nevertheless the work is very toilsome, and as will be seen by the evidence of the surgeon attending Earl Lonsdale's collieries, accidents sometimes occur by the foot slipping off and getting struck by part of the wheel or axle. The leaning position in which they stand is not in itself, I think, injurious; but the work itself strikes one as being palpably unnecessary, and as an objectionable preference of the human body for a mere mechanical process; for which shafts might be, and in some of the inland pits are, used instead. It was indeed stated by one witness, that the use of shafts would be very awkward for the purpose of turning in the foreheads. I believe a very little management would obviate this difficulty.

7. Trappers are employed likewise in nearly all the pits, their work is somewhat augmented by having occasionally two or more doors to attend to, and having to alter checks, so that trains may pass along their proper roads at the dividing places.

8. The trailers are employed chiefly in the smaller and inland collieries. They seldom, however, trail or hurry further than from the foreheads to the"stake", or terminus of the horse road. Their work is decidedly laborious, but so nearly resembling the same employment in Yorkshire, that it is needless to repeat the description of the work. In some few pits the men trail themselves exclusively.

9. The children certainly work longer hours in Cumberland than I have found general in Yorkshire. They seem to work twelve hours habitually, and in some of the inland collieries even longer. Owing to the inefficient power of the drawing-engine in one of these collieries belonging to Mr. Westray, the days work has been extended to 14 or 15 hours; but this cannot be considered other than an accidental circumstance. It is, however, by no means uncommon for pits to work 13 hours a day without a change of hands.

10. In most of Lord Lonsdale's extensive collieries they work night and day, the shift who work the twelve day hours one week working the twelve night hours the succeeding week, and so on alternately. The appearance of the adults in these collieries was remarkably pallid and emaciated. I should attribute this greatly to the system of night working; and there is a probability that the change from night to day hours operates more unfavourably on the health than it would do were they to work altogether at night. In the latter case habit becomes second nature, and sleep as refreshing is obtained by day as by night. Not so when the animal system is subjected to continual change, no habit is formed, and according to the evidence the rest obtained in the day is very deficient; so much so, as to render the night work irksome through the inclination for sleep. The wife generally goes to bed by day with her husband, and so do all the family, the door is often fastened to preserve as much quiet as possible. In some few pits eight hour shifts are worked.

11. The wages of both men and children are very good; they vary from ls to 2s per day for the drivers and trailers, and from 18s to 25s per week for the adult colliers. (1 shilling was equal to 5 new pence).

12. In one colliery I found the wages of the adults amounted to 30s. a week, they being at liberty to work as they pleased. I took pains to ascertain the effect of these high wages on their comforts and conduct. I found that they were no better off than those in other places who earned 20 to 25s. They drink and live more luxuriantly for perhaps two days, and are often ill and off for the rest of the week. I need hardly add that they are fearfully ignorant; and although, strange to say, they will take lessons off an itinerant dancing master, numbers feel no sort of shame in being ignorant of their letters, or bringing up their children without schooling.

13. The accidents within the Whitehaven and Workington collieries were, till within the last eighteen months, most numerous and fearfully fatal. They have arisen chiefly from fire-damp and irruptions of the sea.

14. The accident which occurred in Mr. Curwen's pits near Workington, about two years ago, from an irruption of the sea, was foretold by many. It appears that the seam of coal rose under the sea, so that in working it every step brought the colliers nearer the water. They had proceeded a considerable distance with the workings, I believe nearly two miles, in a direct line from the shore. The salt water is said to have oozed through, and some of the men had heard, the sound of the sea above them. So great was the apprehension, that some of the colliers left their work, and others were only induced to stay by a higher amount of wages. At length the water rushed suddenly in, and though some who were near enough to the entrance escaped, about forty fell victims, and remain to this hour in the pit. The sea, of course, rapidly filled it, and a black gurgling whirlpool for some time marked the aperture and the entrance of the waters at a considerable distance from the shore. The rush of air expelled by the water was so violent that it blew the hats off those who stood near. The blame was attached to Coxton, the steward, who then had charge of the work. He was specially and strongly recommended to Mr. Curwen by Mr. Dunn of Newcastle, and in whom he not unnaturally placed confidence in preference to the reports which reached him from third parties. Coxton would have been torn limb from limb if he had been found by the heart-rent assemblage of the relatives of the sufferers, who thronged to the spot. There cannot be a stronger instance of the danger of trusting the management of coal pits to subordinate and often incompetent persons than this inundation at Workington. It is right to state that the steward was immediately dismissed; and that under the management of the present steward, Mr. Penrice, no accident at any of the pits has occurred worth naming for several months.

15. Prior, however, to the stewardship of Mr. Penrice, another very fatal accident occurred at John Pit, Harrington, belonging to Mr. Curwen, where 24 or 25 persons were burnt to death. At one of Lord Lonsdale's collieries, the William Pit, a similar accident, by which an equal number (23) lost their lives, occurred the year before last (1839). On this occasion Mr. Mitchell, the surgeon, accidentally hit upon carbonate ammonia dissolved in hot water as a remedy to be applied to persons burnt.

16. I feel it right to direct attention to the statement of Mr. Mitchell, to the effect that the coroner has in no instance required him to make Post Mortem examinations of persons crushed to death by falls of roof; without this requirement on the part of the coroner it cannot be done; and this negligence consequently deprives professional men of the information they might otherwise apply to future cases. I applied to the coroner on this point, as well as for a general statement of the accidents which occurred.

17. The following is the answer of the coroner:-

Whitehaven, Carter Lane,

"Sir, 5th August, 1841.

I am sorry I cannot furnish the statement of all the fatal accidents which have come under my cognisance, as coroner, arising from coal-pits, with the nature of the accident, the verdict, the date, and the number of sufferers during the last three years. All the inquisitions are sent every Quarter Sessions to the Clerk of the Peace, with whom they will be found, and the cause of death endorsed on each. Post Mortem examinations can rarely be of any use in deaths occasioned by accidents in coal-pits, for in most cases the person is killed on the spot, especially when it happens, which is the case in most instances, by the roof of the pit falling on the miner.

We have experienced, but not recently, dreadful loss of life by the explosion of inflammable air, but most frequently no one survives to give any account of how the melancholy event occurred.

"I have, &c,
(Signed) "P. Hodgson.

To J. C. Symons, Esq.

18. That Post Mortem examinations can rarely be of any use in cases of deaths by accidents in coal-pits is an assertion which every medical man can confute; the rareness of these examinations is, on the contrary, a most serious evil; and many cases are not improbably lost for want of better insight into the nature of internal injuries, both in the cases of burns and contusions, which Post Mortem examinations can alone supply.

19. A very experienced surgeon in another coal district, in the course of conversation on burns, attributed the difficulty in curing patients to the necessity of giving stimulants to produce re-action after collapse, when the inflammation has been internal, and where stimulants themselves will increase the inflammation; whether the carbonate of ammonia may obviate this evil is a question of great importance. Certain it is, that persons apparently but little burnt, and who are able to walk home from the pits after the accident, above a mile, have subsequently died whilst under medical treatment! Medical science seems to have extended less in this department than any other. From all the evidence I have been able to gather, especially from persons who had been burnt, I should incline to the belief that the injury was internal, whilst the treatment is chiefly external.

20. Accidents from ropes breaking are almost unheard of in Cumberland; nevertheless the ropes used are no larger than in Yorkshire, the pits are double the depth; and the weight drawn is quite as heavy, and often heavier. This can alone be attributed to the system of drawing the baskets up the bratticed shafts without any conductors at all. There is nothing to catch or jerk the ropes, to which the accidents are chiefly referable, which occur so frequently in Yorkshire.

21. The pits are usually well ventilated, and tolerable dry; Lord Lonsdale's are especially. Mr. W. Peile makes some remarks on the theory of ventilation, and the best mode of effecting it, to which I desire to direct your attention.

22. The children are well treated, except as regards the extreme length of time they are confined to the pits; they are in appearance quite as stunted in growth, and present much the same physical phenomena, as those of Yorkshire, comparing, of course those following similar branches of the work. I do not however consider the children, as a body, unhealthy.

23. The morals of the children are very indifferent, and the evidence given is a fair sample of their state of education. They are as ignorant as it is well possible to conceive children to be; nor are the lads of from 13 to 18 years old one jot more informed; but as far as I could ascertain, less so. It is not to be supposed that children confined to 12 hours in a coal-pit can have any opportunities for any sort of education. There are instances of its being previously acquired and retained, and some were selected in Lord Lonsdale's colliery; but this is by no means the rule, and the mental and moral destitution in which the great body of the collier children are growing up in Cumberland is fearfully great.

24. The evidence of the child John Holmes, is a very fair sample of the general state of education among those benighted children :- " I don't go to Sunday School, because I don't like, and I'd rather play. I used to read the Testament. I don't know who Jesus Christ was. I never heard tell of God neither. I am taught to say my prayers, and I say them. I don't know who I pray to !" The education of a parrot is precisely similar, and quite as beneficial to the recipient.

25. The employment of females in coal-pits is rapidly disappearing under the great odium it excites; but very few remain, and only, as far as I learned, in one old colliery of Lord Lonsdale's.

Accidents in the Collieries of Lord Lonsdale, on the Whingill side, out of some hundred men and boys.

From June lst, 1840, to June lst 1841, inclusive.	**Haggers**	**Drivers**	**Trappers**
Crushed by falling of the roof	5	-	2
Crushed causing death	2	1	-
Burnt	11	-	-
Burnt causing death	2	-	-
Fractures	1	3	-
Trifling accidents*	48	14	2
TOTAL	**69**	**18**	**4**

* Trifling accidents which caused the person to be off work between three to twenty days.

I have the honour to be, Gentlemen,

Your very obedient servant,

J.C.SYMONS.

Note: The author's own research found that 13 miners had been killed in the local pits during the above period, and nine more were killed in the months immediately before and after those dates.

Appendix E

List of the Workers in William Pit with Details of Age, Height and Medical Report June 1842

Note: All the trappers and drivers are named in this list, but only a selection of the hundred or more haggers have been named.

TRAPPERS

Name	Age in 1842	Age when first employed	Height	Health
John Blaney	14	12	4' 0½"	Good
Thomas Boyce	11	10	3' 10"	Good
Henry Cotcher	9	8	3' 11"	Good
William Davidson	11	8	4' 4½"	Delicate
George Dawson	13	11	4' 6½"	Takes fits
George Fitzgerald	12	8	4' 7½"	Good
Joseph Fox	12	6	4' 3"	Stunted
James Kennedy	13	12	4' 0"	Delicate
John Kerr	12½	12	4' 6"	Good
Thomas Looney	11	10	4' 2"	Good
Edward McCartney	13	10	4' 7½"	Good
Patrick McLury	11	10	3' 8"	Good
Michael Matthews	10	9	3' 10"	Good
Patrick Merrin	12	11	4' 3½"	Thin
William Steele	10	8½	4' 6"	Good
John Waterson	11	9	4' 1"	Good
William Waterson	15	10	4' 4½"	Good
James Williamson	14	10	4' 7"	Good
John Wood	11	11	4' 2"	Good
Wilkinson Tatters	12	8	4' 3"	Good

DRIVERS

Name	Age in 1842	Age when first employed	Height	Health
Richard Atkinson	16	7	4' 8"	Very good
Robert Blaney	14	12	4' 5"	Good
John Boyce	14	10	4' 41/2"	Good
John Carrick	14	13	4' 10"	Good
Richard Chapelhow	15	10	4' 8"	Good
Daniel Corvin	16	10	4' 0"	Good
Robert Corvin	14	8	4' 5"	Asthma
John Davidson	15	11	4' 8"	Good
John Forsythe	15	121/2	4' 9"	Good
William Gill	18	8	5' 31/2"	Good
George Greers	16	16	4' 11"	Delicate
Peter Henlin	14	13	4' 9"	Good
Thomas Hodgson	14	10	4' 9"	Good
James Kinion	12	9	4' 5"	Good
John McDonald	18	15	5' 4"	Good
James McCourt	16	9	5' 21/2"	Good
Johnathan M'Gliby	23	11	5' 4"	Good
Thomas M'Gliby	19	8	5' 0"	Good
James M'Guire	19	8	5' 3"	Good
William M'Kie	13	9	4' 10"	Good
Frank Milburn	18	8	5' 31/2"	Good
Emanuel Pearson	13	111/2	4' 6"	Good
William Pearson	19	9	4' 8"	Good
Daniel Quinn	16	11	4' 111/2"	Good
George Quinn	13	10	4' 7"	Good
Edward Robson	15	8	4' 11"	Good
James Rothery	16	10	4' 91/2"	Good
John Rothery	18	8	5' 7"	Good
Hugh Smith	14	12	4' 9"	Good
John Steward	13	10	4' 10"	Good
William Stewart	16	7	4' 9"	Good
John Thornton	15	14	4' 111/2"	Good
William Tinkler	17	9	5' 6"	Good
Daniel Wear	13	10	4' 6"	Pale & delicate
Peter Wilson	14	8	4' 6"	Good

HAGGERS

Name	Age in 1842	Age when first employed	Height	Health
George Allan	63	8	5' 6"	Good
William Bainbridge	25	7	5'41/2"	Good
Henry Bigrigg	27	7	5' 6"	Good
Andrew Brocklebank	53	8	5'6"	Good
Hugh Carrick	47	11	5' 101/2"	Good
Hugh Clements	17	12	5' 8"	Good
James Coils	18	10	5' 91/2"	Good
Thomas Copeland	65	10	5' 21/2"	Good
Bernard Corvin	22	10	5' 3"	Delicate
John Cowan	21	10	5' 10"	Very stocky
James Dorian	23	11	5' 2"	Good
Joseph Dorian	21	9	5' 21/2"	Good
Daniel Dunlap	35	11	6' 2"	Good
John Fox	31	9	5' 41/2"	Good
John Fox	24	8	5' 8"	Very stocky
George Geoghanan	35	16	5' 6"	Good
James Glasson	42	22	5' 5"	Good
Thomas Graham	26	9	5' 101/2"	Good
George Holmes	19	10	5' 71/2"	Good
James Hoy	30	14	5' 6"	Good
George Irvin	28	9	5' 4"	Good
Robert Johnston	34	11	5' 61/2"	Good
Frank Lucas	22	12	5' 71/2"	Good
Stephen McCourt	50	16	5' 8"	Good
Stephen McCourt	21	9	5' 9"	Good
John McWhirr	22	11	5' 21/2"	Good
David O'Nail	52	10	5' 4"	Good
William O'Nail	30	11	5' 8"	Very stout
Joseph Peacock	24	11	5' 7"	Good
David Pearson	39	10	5' 61/2"	Good
John Thornton	24	8	5' 41/2"	Good
James Watterson	21	11	5' 5"	Good

Transcribed from a document in The Branch County Record Office, Whitehaven.

Appendix F

GLOSSARY OF MINING TERMS

ADIT - A passage driven into the hillside until it reaches a coal seam. Used for access and drainage.

AFTERDAMP - A mixture of carbon monoxide and other gases resulting from an explosion of firedamp and/or coal dust.

AIR CROSSING - When airways, intake or return, pass directly over or under each other.

AIRWAY - A passage along which a current of air travels.

ATMOSPHERIC ENGINE - In the earliest "steam engines", a partial vacuum was created by condensing steam in the cylinder; atmospheric pressure then powered the movement of the piston. The later true steam engines were more powerful and more economical.

BAIT - Food taken into the pit by the miners. Usually in a tin bait box to protect it from the mice.

BAND - Usually relating to a seam of coal or layer of shale or stone in the strata.

BANKSMAN - The person who controls the movement of the cages up and down the shaft from the shaft top (bank).

BEARMOUTH - Also known as a "Day Hole" an entrance to a coal seam that outcrops at the surface, usually on a hillside.

BELL-PIT - A shallow shaft sunk to reach a coal seam near to the surface. On reaching the seam the coal was extracted around the bottom of the shaft until the roof and sides were in danger of collapsing.

BLACKDAMP - An excess of nitrogen and carbon dioxide found in coal mines, usually in workings with a downward inclination. The gas is produced by the oxidation of coal and timber, the breathing of men and animals, and the burning of flame safety lamps or naked lights. The oxygen in the mine air is reduced which can result in death by suffocation. Also known as **CHOKEDAMP.**

BLOWN-OUT SHOT - When the shot-hole is insufficiently stemmed or given too much burden, (the amount of stone or coal to be blasted) the force of the detonated explosives blow out the stemming and expand into the working which then ignite firedamp or coal dust creating an explosion.

BOGIE - A four wheeled vehicle used for hauling sets of tubs on an endless rope haulage system. Incorporated into the bogie frame is a vice like clip into which the haulage rope is placed. A quick release device is held in position by an upright metal bar (striker). The clip is secured to the rope by screwing the jaws together by means of a screw rod which is turned by a 30" long key known as a 'Poohjah'. The rope is released by striking the striker sideways with the poohjah which allows the clip jaws to open taking the pressure off the rope.

BORD AND PILLAR WORK - The bords were the passages excavated along a coal seam 4 to 5 yards wide. The pillars were the sections of the coal seam that were not removed and left to support the roof. They varied in size depending on the depth of the seam and the strength of the overhead strata, pillars could be between 40 and 100 yards square.

BRATTICE - Wooden boards and thick woven cloth. They were used to partition a shaft or roadway to separate the intake and return air, thus allowing fresh air to circulate through the mine workings.

BUTTY - See **PUFFLER**

CAGE - A steel platform with caged sides and roof, in which men, minerals, and supplies are transported through the shaft.

CHOKEDAMP - See blackdamp.

CLOGS - Miners footwear, consisting of stout leather uppers with a wooden sole. The sole and heel were strengthened with steel cawkers.

COAL MINES ACT - Regulations passed by Parliament governing the safe working of coal mines.

COAL FACE - That part of the mine where the coal is worked; also called the "forehead".

COLLIER - General term for an underground worker. In some pits it refers only to a coal face worker.

COLLIERY - A colliery can consist of one or more pits working the same coal seams. In Whitehaven there were three collieries - Lambhill, Howgill, and Whingill, all owned by Lord Lonsdale.

COURSING THE AIR - A method of ventilating the mines, pioneered by Carlisle Spedding in Saltom Pit, and further developed by his son, James Spedding in 1760. By using brattice and erecting stoppings, the fresh air was circulated around the mine workings dispersing the methane gas.

CAWKERS - Horse shoes; also steel reinforcements nailed to clog soles and heels.

CHOW - A measure of chewing tobacco. One miner would ask his marra for a 'chow'. On a coal face it was kept in the top of his stocking.

CORF - Plural: corves. A basket made of hazel rods, in which coal was conveyed from the coal face to the surface. These were superseded by wooden then steel tubs.

CRANE-MAN - A worker who transferred the corves of coal from the trams trailed from the workings, onto the larger rolleys with a small crane or winch.

CUCKOO SHOT - A shot-hole bored into the roof of the **GOAF**. The hole was fired with the intention of bringing down the roof to provide stone for the building of packs for roof support. This practice was banned after the firing of a cuckoo shot was thought to have caused the 1947 explosion in William Pit .

DAMPS - All mine gasses are called "damps", from the German word 'dampf', meaning a fog or vapour.

DAVY LAMP - A safety lamp invented by Sir Humphrey Davy in 1815.

DEADMAN - A heavy wooden beam 12 to 14 feet in length. Used in place of sleepers when laying track at a junction.

DEPUTY - A colliery official junior to the overman. He is responsible for the safety of the workmen in his district; hence **DEPUTY'S DISTRICT**. A part of the mine shown on the mine plan, assigned to a deputy with the responsibility of carrying out safety inspections, and having the immediate charge of all the workmen and of all operations carried out by them in that district.

DEPUTY'S STATION - A place at the entrance to a "Deputies' District" shown on the Mine Plan. Here the deputy would examine the miners' lamps before allowing them to enter his District to work.

DEVIL - A device used when laying track; it held the sleeper to the track whilst the 'dog' was driven in.

DIRT - A miners term for gas.

DISASTER - When ten or more people are killed in an accident, it is officially termed a disaster.

DOG - A metal spike used for securing the track to the sleeper.

DOORS - Doors are provided underground where persons and vehicles regularly pass between the intake and return roadways. They are always installed in pairs, and sufficient distance apart to enable persons and vehicles to pass through the first door and close it, before passing through the second door.

DOWNCAST SHAFT - The shaft that carries fresh air into the mine workings.

ENGINEMAN - A person who operates the winding apparatus on the surface, (Winding Engineman) or haulage engines underground, (Haulage Engineman).

EYE - 18th and 19th Century miners refered to the shaft as the "Eye of the Pit". The shaft bottom would be called the "Low Eye", the upermost landing the "High Eye", and an intermediate landing the "Middle Eye".

FACE BELT - A conveyor of 24" wide rubber belting. Consisting of a compressed air drive unit, a return roller unit, and intermediate sections with rollers called 'pans', which support the belt. A team of miners called 'pan pullers' would advance the conveyor each day after the coal had been filled out.

FATHOM - Depths of shafts and coal seams were traditionally measured in fathoms. One fathom is equal to six feet or 183 cms.

FAULT - A break in the strata. The miner finds that the seam he is working in is suddenly cut off and lies at a higher or lower level. This displacement is called the 'throw', and if the seam is found at a higher level the miner calls it an upthrow fault, and if at a lower level a downthrow fault.

"FIRES" - A miners term. A pit is said to 'fire' when an explosion takes place. William Pit which produced methane in dangerous quantities was known as a 'fiery' pit.

FIREDAMP - A mixture of air and methane gas. An explosive flammable gas. (See **METHANE**). Firedamp becomes explosive when the methane content is between five and fifteen percent.

FOUL - When air is contaminated by methane gas the, air is deemed to be foul.

FLAT SHEET - A piece of steel sheet half an inch thick and about four feet' square. These are used as a makeshift turn-table, allowing tubs to be got onto another road when there is not a proper junction.

GATE - The name given to the roadway the leads directly to or from the coal face.

GINN - A horse powered winding/pumping machine later replaced by the steam engine. Several of these horse ginns were working near to the bottom of Monkwray Brow in the 18th century, which led to that area being called The Ginns.

GOAF - The area behind the coal face where the coal has been extracted. Sometimes the roof was supported with stone packs, but the modern method is simply to allow the roof to cave in completely.

GRAMPUS - A device used to bend track so that road could be laid round a bend in a haulage road.

GROOM - A person responsible for cleaning and looking after the horses. In 1802 eleven grooms were employed to look after the numerous gin and tram horses working at the Howgill Colliery.

HAGGER or HEWER - The miner who works at the coal face *hagging* or *hewing* the coals.

HAND-FILL - When coal is filled into tubs or onto a conveyor using a shovel. In modern mining coal is mechanically loaded.

HAWK - A custom made hammer and axe combination. One of the blades of a hewing pick is flattened and shaped into an axe, the other blade is shortened and a large nut is welded onto it to form a hammer.

HERCULES - A connector used to re-join the ends of a severed hogger.

HOGGER - A compressed air hose used in connection with compressed air tools.

HORSE - An animal exceeding 14.2 hands in height is classed as a **horse**; if less, it is a **pony**.

HUMIDITY - A measure of the amount of moisture in the mine air.

HURRY - A chute that guided the coals directly into the ship's hold to speed loading.

INUNDATION - When water breaks into the mine workings and floods them.

INBYE - To travel inbye towards the coal faces.

INTAKE AIRWAY - The main roadway taking fresh air into the mine.

INTAKE SIDE. That side of the district or coal face by which the fresh air enters.

JACK ROLL - A simple hand operated winch.

KNUK - The left or right corner of the coal face or heading was referred to as the knuk.

LOCKING - A piece of wood inserted into the spokes of the tub wheels to act as a brake. It was approximately sixteen inches long and two inches square.

LONGWALL FACE - An alternative to Bord and Pillar working. Two headings parallel to each other and 100 yards apart, are driven in the coal seam from the main roadway. At 50 yards the headings are stopped and a face line is formed connecting the two headings, these now become the intake and return roadways for the face. Each hewer is given a measured length of the face to fill out known as his 'stint'. The face advances each day as the coal is filled out by the hewers onto a face conveyor belt. This in turn feeds onto a main conveyor belt which carries the coal outbye to a loading point. From there it is loaded into tubs and sent to the pit bottom by rope haulage.

LOW - An eighteenth-century name for a light or a lit candle.

LOW ROPE - Old gin ropes that were used in place of candles. John Bateman referred to them being used by the miners in Lady Pit in a letter to Lord Lonsdale in 1803.

MARRA - A friend or workmate.

MANHOLE - On a haulage road, a place where a miner can take refuge whilst the sets go past.

METHANE - A gas produced as the coal was formed from decaying vegetable matter, trees and grasses. Mining disturbs the strata and releases the gas. The gas is extremely dangerous because it can be set alight. It is therefore known as a combustible gas and when mixed with air becomes highly explosive.

MINING AGENT - A senior manager responsible to the colliery owner for the working of the colliery.

MONEY - The money referred to in this book is "Old Money" which was superseded by Decimal Currency on 15th February 1971. An old pound was worth 240 old pennies, a shilling 12 old pennies, and half a crown 30 old pennies or 2s and 6d. A new penny is worth 2.4 old pennies.

MOTHER GATE - The intake roadway leading directly to the coal face.

NATIONALISATION - On the January lst 1947 the newly-formed National Coal Board became responsible for the management of Britains' pits.

ONSETTER - The person controlling the movement of the cage from the pit bottom up the shaft. When corves were in use the job was done by females called *Hookers*.

OUTBYE - If a miner is travelling from the coal face towards the shaft he is going outbye.

OUTCROP - When a coal seam is exposed at the surface it referred to as its outcrop.

OVERMAN - An underground official superior to a deputy. Responsible to the undermanager for the deployment of men, production, and transport in one or more districts. A Deputy Overman would be a deputy acting in a temporary capacity as an overman.

PAG - Moist dust on the floor of a roadway forms a clay like substance. A handful of pag could be used to stick a candle to a pit prop.

PACKERS - The miners who built stone walled packs filled with rubble, to support the roof in the goaf as the coal face advanced.

PAN PULLER - The miners who dismantled and re-laid the face conveyor in it's new run, after the coal had been filled out by the hewers.

PIT - A loosely used term in coal mining. It could refer to a pit, a single shaft of a mine, or even an entire colliery.

PIT BOTTOM - The lowest landing place in the shaft.

POOHJAH - A device used to tighten the screw on a bogie. A 36" long iron bar fitted with square spanner head which was placed over the screw of the bogie, the haulage worker would pull on the poohjah to tighten the jaws of the bogie clip onto the haulage rope. He would also use it to release the rope from the clip by striking the striker. (See **BOGIE**).

POP SHOT - An illegal shot fired in a very short hole.

PROP - A length of stout timber, it's length depending on the height of the seam in which it was to be used. A pair of props would be set under a horizontal wooden bar called a "Headtree" to support the roof as the roadway advanced.

PUFFLER - On a coal face the hewers would choose one of their members to act as their spokesman. He would measure out each of the hewers' "stints" and discuss any problems that may arise with the officials. At the week-end he would assist the overman when the weekly drivage measurement was taken. He would also receive the "Big Cheque" the day before payday, which showed what coal had been hewn on that face, and the total amount earned by the team. Prior to 1842, the puffler would be given the team's wages and would arrange to meet them at a public house where he would pay them individually. In the 19th Century the Puffler was known as the **"BUTTY"**.

PULLEY - A wheel with a double flanged rim over which a rope passes. It can be suspended from the roof in a bracket as is used in an overhead haulage system, or supported on the floor in a square metal or wooden frame

PUTTER - Another name for a trailer. Miners who came from the Newcastle area to work in the Whitehaven pits would call a trailer a putter.

RAKE - When a trailer completes one journey from the coal heading to the haulage road and back, he has completed one rake.

RIPPER - A miner employed to enlarge the 'gates' as the coal face advanced. Also known as a 'brusher'.

ROAD - The steel track laid in the haulage roads on which the tubs and trams ran was always referred to as the road. When a tub was derailed it was said to be "off the road".

ROADWAY - A passage in the mine, a haulage road.

ROBBING OUT - When a district was to be abandoned, the remaining pillars left in to support the roof were systematically robbed' by reducing their size. This was a dangerous practice and if not properly managed could lead to roof falls, and large quantities of firedamp from the goaf being forced into the roadways creating the threat of an explosion.

ROLLEY - A carriage used to transport the corves outbye. A Galloway pony might only manage to pull a one corve rolley, whereas a horse would manage a four or five corve rolley.

ROLLEY ROAD - The underground roadway used for the movement of rollys to and from the workings.

ROLLEY-WAY-MAN - A person responsible for looking after the maintenance of a rolley-way.

ROPE - Until the mid nineteenth century haulage and winding ropes were made from hemp. In 1874, at St Lawrence Colliery, the first practical application of steel rope was used on a horse gin for raising coals.

SCOGGERS - Stockings with feet cut off. These were worn over the stockings and pulled down over the tops of the clogs/boots to prevent small pieces of stone or coal getting inside them.

SCUTCH - A stout metal bar 16" long with a circular handle thrust between the spokes of a tub to serve as a braking device.

SEAM - A stratum of coal in a coal mine. In the Whitehaven pits the seams worked were the Metal Band, Bannock, Main, and Six Quarters seams.

SHAFT - A vertical entrance into a mine from the surface.

SLYPING - The illegal removal of the coal from the supporting pillars - a serious offence.

SNUFF BOX - The return roller end of a face conveyor. Coal carried into the roller would be crushed into a fine powder by the belt. Lads were employed to keep it clean to prevent the belt sticking.

STAPLE SHAFT - A vertical shaft within a mine connecting one level to another.

SHIFT - A group of miners who worked for a specific period. The period of time worked by such a group. In the eighteenth century, miners worked twelve hour shifts split into *night* and *day* shifts, When the shifts were reduced to eight hours, miners would work *first*, (day) *back*, (afternoon) and *night* shifts.

SHOT - The detonating of explosives in a pre-drilled hole.

SHOT FIRER - An official with the sole task of the firing of shots. A deputy could fire shots but no more than eight during his shift.

SKITE - A local variation of the word slide. When a locking or scutch was inserted into the spokes of a tub, it could be 'skited' down an incline.

SPEDDING MILL or STEEL MILL - Invented by Carlisle Spedding of Whitehaven. This contrivance produced a shower of sparks by turning the hardened steel wheel of the mill against a flint held by the operator. These were still in use at the William Pit until the arrival of the Davy Lamp in 1816.

STAITH - A large bunker that was used to store coals prior to being loaded onto the ships. Whitehaven had a large one on the West Strand.

STAKE - The furthest point reached by the horse roads; beyond this, the corves were moved by trailers from the **FOREHEADS.**

STOPPING - A method of sealing off a roadway leading to a disused district. The roadway is stowed with at least five meters of rubble, then faced with brick.

STRATA - The layers of rock through which a coal mine is sunk. A single layer is a *stratum.*

TAILGATE - The return roadway leading directly from the coal face.

THIRL - A small passage connecting one roadway to another.

TRAILER - The miner who pushes the tub or tram from the coal heading to the haulage road.

TRIAL - An exploratory roadway driven into a previously unworked area of the mine.

TUB - A four wheeled rectangular vehicle used for transporting coal or materials underground. Firstly made of wood then steel, tubs could hold up to one ton of coal, depending on the height of the roadway.

UPCAST - The shaft through which air is expelled from the pit after ventilating the workings.

VENTILATION - The controlled circulation of air through the mine workings.

VIEWER - An old term for a mine manager. An under viewer was an under-manger.

WASTER - An old term for a deputy. The waster would inspect the workings before the workmen were allowed to enter.

WORKINGS - The part of the mine where coal production is or has taken place. The excavated areas underground.

Appendix G

William Pit

The Cost of Coal

Should brave men die, should kinsfolk cry, so be the cross to bear.
No earthly writ served on that pit, would set the balance square.

The sun blessed sky held spirits high, those miners to that mine.
Not kith nor kind they left behind, beheld a trouble sign.

But tragedy was deemed to be, among the dust and grit.
For knew not they what mischief lay, within the William Pit.

T'was not God's grace upon that face, upon that face alas.
Amidst the coal was 'Satans Dole', a pocket filled with gas.

For whom can tell the road to hell, to heaven or despair.
Mid dust and spew the devil knew, explosion rent the air.

No holding fast his evil blast, as coal dust vent his spite.
A savage foe to lend a blow, with devastating might.

The whipped-up dust produced a gust, destructive in it's bent.
A channelled force to run the course, until at last was spent.

That ripping ball laid waste to all, that was within it's rake.
And in its pass the after gas, would follow in it's wake.

On knees stand tall on stomach crawl, in murk and firedamp.
And darkness broken by a light, that be a miners lamp.

Oh sons of toil thy lamp of oil, would burn until the flame.
Proclaimed a hue of dreaded blue, proclaiming gas had came.

Lay down to sleep safe in God's keep, their mining days be o'er
Within their name there lay no shame, no others could be more.

Ask not what a miner's got, ask what he had to give.
Descend in cage to earn a wage, and so a life to live.

Nor ask of why brave men would die, but ask the price of coal.
The 'William' cursed was not the first, though helped to swell the toll

No more their role to hag the coal, no more to sweat and hew.
Deep underground those miners found, the cost of coal in lieu.

No pounds and pence could recompense, kindred folk or kind.
Damned blasted coal thou took thy toll, the price for being mined.

Not by the ton thy fee was won, not by the cube or yard.
Thy price in blood be claimed it would, with not a scant regard.

Let's remember with pride all those who died, down in that man-made hell.
Five score and four who'd toil no more, and those who'd live to tell.

Their darkest night mark well that site, and count the cost of coal.
Though wage may pay the toil of day, it cannot pay the soul.

Appendix H

Closure of Pits During the 20th Century

This list cannot be regarded as definitive. There are almost certainly omissions, and some of the dates are open to question. A number of very small concerns (such as drift mines worked by a handful of men) are included as well as substantial pits whose operations are reasonably well documented. Sometimes a new shaft might have been sunk to exploit the same area as an earlier one - Croft Pit, for example, closed as a pit in 1903, but its shaft and air-ways were maintained to ventilate the Ladysmith Pit, which was completed in the same year. Similarly, a shaft working higher bands might have been later extended to reach deeper ones, so leading to confusion over the date of sinking. In other cases adjacent pits might later have been amalgamated, causing problems with dating or naming. Finally, it must be born in mind that a colliery consists of two or more pits worked as a single concern; the date of closure of an individual pit may not correspond to the closure of a colliery.

1903	Croft Pit, Whitehaven
1903	Cammerton No.1 Pit
1908	Asby Colliery
1910	Elen Pit, Gilcrux
1911	Cammerton No. 2 Pit
1913	Un-specified pit in Wythemoor area (sunk 1909-1911)
1914	Ellenborough Colliery
1914	Bertha Pit, Broughton Moor
1917	Brayton Knowe Pit (sunk 1902)
1921	Alice Pit, Oatlands, near Maryport
1921	St Helens No.2, Siddick
1924	Bertha Pit, Broughton Moor
1928	Allhallows Pit, Maryport
1928	Mill Drift, Dearham
1929	Mill Pit, Dearham
1930	Bolton Pit, Maryport
1931	Ladysmith Pit, Whitehaven
1932	Buckhill, Maryport
1932	Harrington No.12 (sunk 1921-22)
1932	Wellington Pit, Whitehaven
1933	Brayton Domain No.4

1934	Oatlands Pit, Distington (sunk 1880)
1942	Brayton Domain No.5
1943	Westmoor No.1 & No.2 (sunk c. 1940)
1943	Oughterside Pit
1950	Birkby & Allbright Colliery, Dearham
1951	Moorside Drift, Dean Moor
1952	Ellenbank Drift, Maryport
1955	William Pit, Whitehaven (sunk 1805)
1959	Clifton Pit
1959	Gillhead Pit
1961	Walkmill, Moresby (sunk 1877-79).
1963	Harrington No.11 (sunk 1916)
1964	Siddick Pit, Workington. (No. 3 shaft sunk 1877, deepened 1889)
1966	Risehow, Maryport (sunk 1913)
1966	St. Helens, Workington
1968	Harrington No.10 (sunk 1910-11)
1973	Solway Colliery, Workington (sunk 1937)
1986	Haig Pit, Whitehaven (sunk 1914-1918)

Owners or Lessees

1630 - 1644
Sir Christopher Lowther of Whitehaven (1611-1644)
Took charge of Whitehaven Estate c. 1630

1644 - 1706
Sir John Lowther of Whitehaven (1642-1706)
Estate run by Trustees until he came of age, 1653.
Bequeathed estate to his younger son, James

1706 - 1755/56
Sir James Lowther of Whitehaven (1673-1735)
Died without heir. Estate bequeathed to William, of Holker, who himself died the following year and was succeeded by Sir James, of Maulds Meaburn

1756 - 1802
Sir James Lowther of Maulds Meaburn (1736-1802)
Created 1st Earl of Lonsdale, 1784, but died without heir so title extinguished on his death. Estate bequeathed to Sir William.

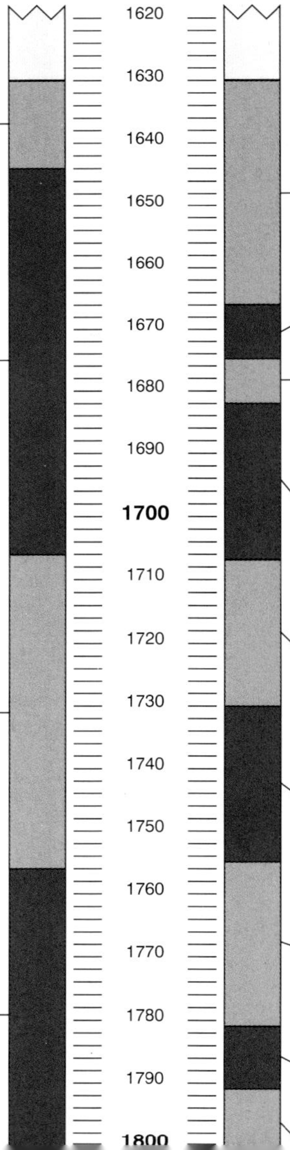

Mining Stewards / Managers

1630 - 1666
Various Estate Stewards responsible, amongst other things, for supervising coal workings

1666 - 1675
Thomas Jackson Mining Steward

1675 - 1682
Three Colliery Stewards in quick succession:-
Henry Addison (for 4 months only);
Richard Bettesworth (1675-77)
Laurence Braithwaite (1677-1682)

1682 - 1707
John Gale. Responsible for managing estate AND mines. Dismissed, 1707

1707 - 1730
John Spedding. Replaced Gale in 1707; he remained Estate Steward after that time, whilst his brother Carlisle took charge of the mining operations.

1730 - 1755
Carlisle Spedding. Killed by explosion of fire damp, 1755. Succeeded by son, James.

1755 - 1781
James Spedding. When his uncle John (above) died in 1758, James took charge of Estate in addition to mines. Resigned.

1781 - 1791
John Bateman General Manager of mines.
Dismissed

1802 - 1844
Sir William Lowther of Swillington (17?? -1844)
Became 1st Lord Lonsdale (by 2nd creation), 1807
Succeeded by son, William

1844 - 1872
William Lowther (1776 -1882) Created 2nd Earl
Succeeded by nephew, Henry

1872 - 1876
Henry Lowther (1818-1876) Created 3rd Earl
Succeeded by son, St. George Henry

1876 - 1880
St. George Henry Lowther (1855-1882) 4th Earl
Two years before his death, mining interests leased
thus ending the Lowthers' direct control of the pits

1880 - 1913
Whitehaven Pits leased to Bain & Co.

1913 - 1933
New lease - Whitehaven Colliery Co.

1933 -1935
Pits Closed

1935 -1937
Leased to Priestman Whitehaven Collieries

1937 - 1947
Leased to Cumberland Coal Co. (Whitehaven)

1947
Nationalisation; pits owned by National Coal Board

1986
Haig Pit closed - the last shaft mine in Cumbria

1810 1820 1830 1840 1850 1860 1870 1880 1890 **1900** 1910 1920 1930 1940 1950 1960 1960 1970 **1986**

1791 - 1802
Thomas Wyley. Dismissed 1802

1802 - 1811
John Bateman re-appointed. Again Dismissed

1811 - 1847
John Peile. Retired

1847 - 1867
Peter Bourne. Retired

1867 - 1880
Team of managers:-
TE Forster, GB Forster & TG Hurst

1880 - 1947
Managers appointed by successive private leeses

1947 - 1986
Managers appointed by National Coal Board